D.H. LAWRENCE

A Study of the Short Fiction

Also available in Twayne's Studies in Short Fiction Series

Twayne's Studies in Short Fiction

Gordon Weaver, General Editor
Oklahoma State University

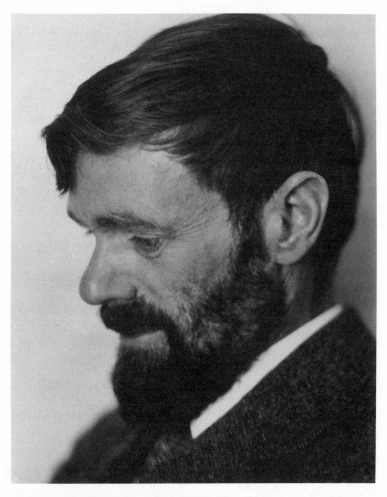

D.H. Lawrence, 1924
Photography by Edward Weston, ©1981 Center for Creative Photography,
Arizona Board of Regents

D. H. LAWRENCE

A Study of the Short Fiction

Weldon Thornton
University of North Carolina at Chapel Hill

TWAYNE PUBLISHERS • NEW YORK
Maxwell Macmillan Canada   Toronto
Maxwell Macmillan International
New York   Oxford   Singapore   Sydney

Twayne's Studies in Short Fiction Series, No. 54

Copyright © 1993 by Twayne Publishers

Twayne Publishers
Macmillan Publishing Company
866 Third Avenue
New York, New York 10022

Maxwell Macmillan Canada, Inc.
1200 Eglinton Avenue East
Suite 200
Don Mills, Ontario M3C 3N1

Library of Congress Cataloging-in-Publication Data
Thornton, Weldon.
  D.H. Lawrence: a study of the short fiction/Weldon Thornton.
  p. cm. -- (Twayne's studies in short fiction)
  Includes bibliographical references (p.) and index.
  ISBN 0-8057-0862-6
  1. Lawrence, D. H. (David Herbert), 1885-1930--Criticism and interpretation. 2. Short story. I. Title. II. Series.
PR6023.A93Z928 1993
823' . 912--dc20   93-25540
                                                        CIP

10 9 8 7 6 5 4 3 2 1

Printed in the United States of America

For Amy, Erin, and Diane
the new women in my life

Contents

Preface

This book explores the distinctive achievement of Lawrence's short stories and the challenges they present to the reader. Although a great deal has been written about the stories, critics still fail to approach them in a manner that does justice to their great subtlety, depth, and power. Criticism continues to be vitiated and led astray by inappropriate reference to supposed biographical connections to the stories and by invocation of certain themes the stories are presumed to illustrate. If, as Lawrence himself advised, we heed the tale not the author, and permit the stories to speak for themselves, they offer an amazing array of explorations of diverse human situations.

My discussions of individual stories are intended both to interpret the stories and to illustrate the claims I make about stumbling blocks to our reading of Lawrence's works and about the unappreciated quality of many of his stories. While my interpretations of individual stories exemplify my claims about point of view, contextuality, and the proper bases of character evaluation in Lawrence's fiction, my readings are not programmatic. My underlying aim is to do justice to stories that are subtle and elusive and that often have not been given the close attention they deserve. Certainly, there are some failures among Lawrence's stories, but the longer I work with them the more cautious I become about dismissing any one of them as superficial or about assuming that a story is merely an illustration of some recognized Lawrencean theme. More than once I have been surprised to realize the fine qualities of a story I had disdained, led by students who somehow tuned in to the story better than I had.

This volume makes no attempt to provide information about every story Lawrence wrote, or to provide a review of the secondary criticism. Freed from those obligations by the guidelines of this series and by the existence (or immanence) of other books that do those things, my aim here is to take a closer, more detailed look at a small number of selected stories.[1] Our understanding of D. H. Lawrence's short stories has in some respects suffered because several books have attempted brief accounts of virtually all of the stories—for example, the books of E. W. Tedlock, Jr., Kingsley Widmer, F. B. Pinion's *D. H. Lawrence Companion,* and even to some extent Janice Harris's intelligent book (see my bibliography). Such attempts, impressive in scope as they are, invite simplifications, regarding the stories as having some biographical key, as illustrating some abstractable Lawrencean theme, or as epitomizing some phase or category of his work. By attending carefully to a smaller number of Lawrence's stories, some of them neglected, I can illustrate the surprising quality of these stories and encourage more careful attention to others.

Paradoxically, another stumbling block to keeping our eye on the meanings of Lawrence's works is the daunting volume of biographical and textual information now available through the new editions of his works and the letters, and the biography being written as this book nears completion. Especially for those of us who are interested in Lawrence's life and thought, not just his literary works, this daunting array of new information makes it harder to remember that the meanings of these works involve more than their biographical or ideational context, and that these distinctive meanings are the heart of why we value Lawrence as we do.

Lawrence's fictional works show little regard for the categories that scholars employ: short story, novella, novel. I have confined myself here to the short stories, finding more there than I could possibly do justice to in so brief a span. This means that the novellas, wonderful as several of them are, lie beyond my scope.

Note

1. Martin F. Kearney is preparing a volume on Lawrence to be titled *A Reader's Guide to the Short Stories of D.H. Lawrence.* Several volumes of the Cambridge edition that include short stories have already appeared and others are forthcoming; these volumes include reliable information about the composition and publishing history of each story, as well as an established text and textual and explanatory notes. A great deal of relevant information can be found in John Worthen's first volume of the biography of Lawrence published in 1991. As this book nears completion, the second and third volumes are still being written by Mark Kinkead-Weekes and David Ellis, respectively.

Acknowledgments

This book owes most to the many students who have written papers on the short stories of D. H. Lawrence for me over the past several decades. The responses that their ideas evoked in me form much of the substance of the book.

I wish also to thank my several colleagues who have read parts of this manuscript and have argued with me about this wonderful, challenging writer. I owe special thanks to James C. Cowan, who made this project possible.

My thanks also to Frances Coombs whose assistance in preparing the manuscript was indispensable.

The first section of this book, "D. H. Lawrence and the Short Story," is a revised version of my essay, "D. H. Lawrence," which appeared in *The English Short Story 1880–1945: A Critical History*, edited by Joseph M. Flora (Twayne Publishers/Macmillan, 1985). Copyright © 1985 by G. K. Hall.

An earlier version of my discussion of "England, My England" appeared in the Fall 1983 issue of the *D. H. Lawrence Review* and is reprinted here by permission of the *Review* and of Dennis Jackson, editor.

Acknowledgment for right to reprint material from the works and letters of D. H. Lawrence is made to Laurence Pollinger Ltd. and the Estate of Frieda Lawrence Ravagli.

Part 1

THE SHORT FICTION

D. H. Lawrence and the Short Story

D. H. Lawrence is celebrated for having written some of the finest stories in our language, and virtually every anthology of short fiction includes an example of his work. Several of his most frequently anthologized stories have been discussed extensively and are accepted as classics of the form. Yet of the more than 50 short stories Lawrence wrote, many fine ones have not been fully appreciated for their psychological and artistic subtlety, and the distinctive aims and devices of these stories have yet to be adequately understood. This lack of understanding persists primarily because Lawrence conforms not at all to the post-Flaubertian, modernist image of the artistic craftsman. His rejection of the aesthetic ideal of authorial effacement and dispassion suggests to some critics that he lacks artistic control and that his work is vitiated by his personal involvement in the stories. As a result, readers still habitually approach his stories with certain debilitating assumptions about the nature and quality of their art. But paradoxically Lawrence is—especially in the presentation of his characters' psychological states and relationships—more radically innovative and subtly demanding than practitioners of the "received experimentalism" represented by more conventional stream-of-consciousness storytelling.[1]

Lawrence's best work calls into play psychological dimensions and aesthetic sensibilities not fully explored by most modernist literature. It requires of the reader a willingness to go to the works free from preconceptions about what constitutes "good art" and from the presumption that the stories "illustrate" ideas expressed in Lawrence's essays or letters. Mark Schorer, for instance, in his influential essay "Technique as Discovery," presumes that the mode of authorial presence espoused by Henry James, Conrad, and Joyce is the only defensible one and that Lawrence's departure from it in *Sons and Lovers* and other works is a sign of his technical failure.[2] Such misapplication of modernist aesthetic criteria, no less than criticism overly concerned with biography or "doctrine," interferes with a full appreciation of the technical skill, the psychological depth, and the thematic subtlety of Lawrence's work. The fervor and ubiquity of Lawrence's expository comments in various essays and introductions have encouraged critics to take an "ideational approach" to the works. Thus even critics who admire Lawrence sometimes seem surprised to discover that a story does not simply illustrate some presumed Lawrencean doctrine; however, they seldom go on to analyze the methods by which Lawrence achieves this subtlety.[3] Through my readings of several of Lawrence's stories I hope to demonstrate the unappreciated skill and subtlety of their art.

Though Lawrence is recognized as a master of the form, his short stories bear few generic similarities to those of other short story writers before him or after. Lawrence did read and in some cases (temporarily) admired the writers who established the "modern" short story—Poe, Flaubert, Chekhov, Maupassant, Joyce, Mansfield, and Hemingway—but they had little tangible influence on him, nor, in the case of more recent writers, he on them. These writers emphasize verbal economy, skillful contrivance of some single effect, and careful preparation for the "epiphanic" moment. They aspire to refine the author out of existence, and abjure "telling" in favor of "showing." Their stories focus upon a crucial turning point in the life of a character, often manifested in a clear realization on the character's part. Frank O'Connor quotes a line from Gogol's "The Overcoat" to epitomize such an epiphanic revelation: "and from that day forth, everything was as it were changed and appeared in a different light to him."[4] In Lawrence's stories, in contrast, the narrative voice often assumes a palpable presence, the narrative is not so sharply focused upon a single effect, and the presentation admits of few such clearly cognitive epiphanies. More often the story's ending depicts characters struggling to come to terms with their own feelings or even their own acts.

Although the modernist pedigree in short fiction has been held in the highest critical esteem, there is another important species of story, indigenous to Britain and represented in the works of Stevenson, Hardy, Kipling, and, more recently, A. E. Coppard and H. E. Bates. Stories in this tradition, perhaps better called "tales," differ from their modernist counterparts in several ways. They are characteristically of broader scope and more diffuse presentation, often running far longer than the length sanctioned by Maupassant's brief paradigm. (Examples of such longer, more diffuse tales include Stevenson's "The Beach at Falesá," Hardy's "The Distracted Preacher," Kipling's "The

Man Who Would Be King," Coppard's "My Hundredth Tale," and many of Bates's works.) Stories in this tradition are more likely to involve a narrator, either playing some active role in events or functioning as storyteller. The events recounted may cover several years; plot is important and sometimes complex. Characters, on the other hand, are less sharply focused upon, tending to assume their places in some larger scheme of action and setting. And within this countertradition there are of course variations—from Stevenson's penchant for the violent and outré to Coppard's more subdued realism.

Lawrence has more in common with the storytellers of this mode (especially if Hardy is included) than he does with the mainline modernists, but his stories do involve some significant differences from these tales. In a story by Lawrence, plot is never the primary interest, and the authorial voice, though undeniably present, rarely emerges as a tangible persona or character. In Lawrence's stories the conception of character, of personality, is more complex; the focus of interest is more intensely psychological—especially concerning conflicts within and among the characters; and the style is more "poetic," that is, it involves distinctive rhythms and repetitions and imagery, than in most tales.[5]

Critical studies of the short story have done little to place Lawrence in reference to any particular school, or to pin down writers and stories that most influenced him. Walter Allen's *The Short Story in English*, for instance, consistently praises Lawrence's technique and insight and ranks him "second only to Kipling in English writing."[6] But other than briefly comparing "The White Stocking" with Chekhov's "The Darling," Allen makes little effort to determine his place in the history of the form. Similarly, T. O. Beachcroft praises Lawrence's stories, particularly the "remarkable contribution" the stories of *The Prussian Officer* volume made "to the form as well as the substance of short stories," yet fails to discuss Lawrence's predecessors or followers in the genre, or to analyze his contribution to it, remarking that at times "one feels he [Lawrence] is simply not interested in the form of the story."[7] Lawrence scholars too have had little to say about the influences on Lawrence as a writer of short stories, despite the evidence both in his letters and in Jessie Chamber's *D. H. Lawrence: A Personal Record*, regarding his attentive reading of works by Balzac, Maupassant, Zola, Gorky, Hardy, as well as those written by his contemporaries and appearing in the *English Review*.[8] While several critics have pointed out affinities specifically with George Eliot or Thomas Hardy, they have made no case for influence on Lawrence's practice of the short story.[9]

Only Keith Cushman in "The Young D. H. Lawrence and the Short Story" explores Lawrence's origins as a writer of short fiction and documents what Lawrence had to say about the short story genre.[10] Cushman designates Gorky and Maupassant as "the most important early influences on Lawrence the short story writer," and says that, at least for a time, Lawrence espoused realism and "saw himself as belonging to this 'school'" (101)—though Cushman weakens the thrust of this claim when he counts Hardy as a realist simply on the basis of his desire to make "fiction speak directly to the reality of human experience" (102). Cushman's claim for Lawrence as a realist rests on ambiguous statements by Jessie Chambers that Lawrence was thrilled by Maupassant's technique, and most of all on a letter written by Lawrence to Louie Burrows in which Lawrence recommends reading the *English Review* as "the best possible way to get into touch with the new young school of realism" (101). Cushman assumes the realism Lawrence refers to is that of Maupassant and Gorky.

A closer look at the context of Lawrence's remark and at the *English Review* shows that what Lawrence means by realism is something much broader than the practice of those two writers. In the letter to Burrows, Lawrence describes the *English Review:*

> It is very fine, and very "new." There you will meet the new spirit at its best.... It is the best possible way to get into touch with the new young school of realism, to take the *English Review*. In this month's issue [October 1909], there is a particularly fine story, [Anne Douglas Sedgwick's] "The Nest"—such a one as you would find nowhere but in the *English*, and a magnificent story.... I return you the "Goose Fair"—you may as well keep it entirely. If I had it I should write it out again, and vivify in places: but you will use your own discretion.... But pray do not write *too* romantically: write as near to life as possible. You needn't be pessimistic or cynical, but it is always best to be true. The *English Review* is finely truthful, on the whole.[11]

This letter suggests that what Lawrence means by realism stands at some remove from the school of Maupassant. Cushman himself puzzles over Lawrence's admiration for Sedgwick's "The Nest" and acknowledges that it "is certainly radically unlike the short stories of

Gorky [and] Maupassant" (108). Indeed, Sedgwick's story is undoubtedly much closer to what I have described as a "tale" than a "modern" short story. Furthermore, although Lawrence does advise Louie Burrows not to write "*too* romantically" in "Goose Fair," he then goes on to warn against pessimism or cynicism—elements common in Maupassant—in favor of simply being true to life.

In light of Lawrence's reference to the October 1909 issue of the *English Review* and his persistent association of that magazine with the "new" mode, it is revealing to examine an essay by J. A. Hobson called "The Task of Realism" that appeared in that very issue.[12] Using the term in neither a strictly literary nor a philosophical sense, Hobson calls for a new and more comprehensive approach to experience; the "fuller" realism he advocates takes into account "creative or interpretive hypotheses," and can thus be distinguished from "the cruder realism whose only facts were hard and dead" (553). Hobson sees "that realism which to-day is struggling for positive expression" (551) as moving a step beyond its "early inroads" into the fictional, poetic, and dramatic works of "Tolstoy, Zola, Ibsen, Shaw, Brieux" (549–50), and while he acknowledges that "[a]t first sight realism may appear an extremely inadequate word to express that striving of head and heart which is replacing the dissipation and distraction of the earlier rationalism" (552), he can find no other adequate term. In a closing statement, perhaps echoed in Lawrence's praise of the *Review* in his letter to Louie Burrows, Hobson calls on the magazine to champion this new realism, hoping that "those who accept the view that experiments in collective self-consciousness, as a means of accelerating and directing the 'urge of the world' towards human enlightenment and well-being, are likely to yield great results, will recognize that a rendering of realism in many fields of thought and art is the most profitable use for such a *Review*" (554).

Julian Moynahan has discussed Lawrence's attitude toward realism and finds it to be skeptical: "It is important for us to understand how energetically and explicitly Lawrence took issue with the assumptions and techniques of the Flaubertian mode of prose realism which, on the whole, have dominated twentieth-century fiction from the early stories of Joyce to the latest well-made *New Yorker* piece of today."[13]

Moynahan goes on to quote from Lawrence's 1913 piece "German Books—Thomas Mann," in which he describes Mann as "the last sick sufferer from the complaint of Flaubert."[14] He points out that Lawrence's persistent and continuing criticisms of realism were based "not on caprice and ignorance, but on wide thoughtful reading in the works of great continental realists, French, Russian, Italian, and German, more often than not in the original languages" (XV), and he quotes Lawrence's disavowal of self-effacement on the grounds that it is "self-conscious, and any form of emotional self-consciousness hinders a first-rate artist" ("Preface" to Giovanni Verga's *Cavalleria Rusticana*, in *Phoenix*, 248). He points out as well that Lawrence criticizes realism for its "submissiveness and abjectness," and quotes his statement that

> Realism is just one of the arbitrary views man takes of man. It sees us all as little ant-like creatures toiling against the odds of circumstance, and doomed to misery. It is a kind of aeroplane view. It becomes the popular outlook, and so today we actually are, millions of us, little ant-like creatures toiling against the odds of circumstance and doomed to misery; until we take a different view of ourselves. (Moynahan, xvi, quoting from an alternate version of Lawrence's "Introduction" to *Mastro-Don Gesualdo*)[15]

Even while presenting his arguments for Lawrence as realist, Keith Cushman notes aspects of his work, notably the "rare emotive power," that separate him from the mode of Maupassant and Gorky, and finally Cushman admits "the question of Lawrence's relation to the tradition of the short story remains curiously elusive" (Cushman, "The Young D. H. Lawrence," 109). This elusiveness is in part due to the very nature of the short story; of all modern literary forms, it is the least determined by literary convention, the most likely to be all things to all people. The link of the short story to the perennial human inclination to present experience in brief narrative accounts is borne out by A. E. Coppard who, in the "Foreword" to his *Collected Tales*, contrasts the novel, an art form with a clear distinct pedigree, with the short story, "an ancient art originating in the folk tale." "Cut a person off from all contact with tales," Coppard observes, "and he will assuredly begin to invent some."[16] So while theoreticians may present one or another mode of the short story as normative or paradigmatic (for example, those of Maupassant or Chekhov), such modes by no means exhaust the possibilities.[17]

A more important reason for our difficulties in trying to pigeonhole Lawrence's stories lies in his distinctive mind and talent, and especially in his attitudes toward and his uses of art. Lawrence, more than most other writers, used his writings in all genres to engage and explore experience, to work through his own nascent, tentative ideas and feelings. He empathizes so thoroughly with his characters' situations as to emerge from the writing having experienced something. Most of us can develop no alternative to living by the trial-and-error method to come to terms with experience; even most writers are too concerned for their image or their reputation, or with the place of their work in the literary tradition or its acceptability to the reading public, to write in a way that is truly exploratory. But for D. H. Lawrence, the act of writing always was an act of exploration, of working through feelings and problems.[18] The author's well-known statement in a 26 October 1913 letter to Arthur McLeod bears this out: "one sheds ones sicknesses in books—repeats and presents again ones emotions, to be master of them."[19]

This exploratory quality in Lawrence's work does not imply any lack of authorial control; it is simply that the control he exercises is intuitive and holistic rather than narrowly cognitive. Lawrence judges the rightness of an evolving work not by its conformity to some preconceived notion or traditional form, but by his informed intuition about whether the work is on the right track, whether it is leading somewhere fruitful. This is the gist of several of Lawrence's comments to correspondents about his works in progress, especially during 1913 and 1914 when his talent was evolving so quickly and he was gaining confidence and skill in the distinctive modes of his art. In a 23 April 1913 letter to Arthur McLeod, for instance, he says of *The Sisters* (later *The Rainbow/Women in Love*): "I am doing a novel which I have never grasped. Damn its eyes, there I am at page 145, and I've no notion what it's about. I hate it. F[rieda] says it is good. But it's like a novel in a foreign language I don't know very well—I can only just make out what it is about" (*Letters*, 2:544). The exploratory nature of his writing is reflected too in his comment in "Morality and the Novel" that "when the novelist puts his thumb in the scale, to pull down the balance to his own predilection, that is immorality"—in other words, he violates the integrity of his purpose.[20] For Lawrence, art can give form to experience, can give it a distinctive ordering at once affective and cognitive and thus more subtle and comprehensive than any form based upon sheer conceptualization. But this capacity of art to be a means of exploring the often fearful future is frustrated if the writer loses faith in what he is doing and uses the story or novel merely to illustrate some preconceived idea.

This exploratory motive of his art explains why Lawrence's works exist in so wide an array of lengths and of types; this variety arises not from his indifference to form or genre, but from his need for different lengths and modes to explore situations or problems of different scope or depth. And while the novel can by virtue of its greater length deal with life issues of larger scope and greater depth—which is why for Lawrence it is "the one bright book of life"[21]—his various short stories and novelettes are the appropriate mode and vehicle for their subjects.

Lawrence's understanding of literary form is a concomitant of his view of art as exploratory. Often in his letters—again, especially during 1913 and 1914—he comments on the form of some work he is reading or writing: in these comments he distinguishes between form as received aesthetic convention, and form as the appropriate manifestation of the writer's subject and purposes. In his review on Thomas Mann (written in May 1913), he faults both contemporary German literature and the school of Flaubert for craving a logical aesthetic form that attempts to fix "the definite line of the book." "But, can the human mind," Lawrence asks, "fix absolutely the definite line of a book, any more than it can fix absolutely any definite line of action for a living being?" ("German Books: Thomas Mann," in *Phoenix*, 308).

Little interested in form as an aesthetic convention, he is concerned about form as the most appropriate mode of expression. In a letter of 24 December 1912 to Ernest Collings, Lawrence makes just this distinction, speaking first of the difficulty of finding "exactly the form one's passion . . . wants to take," and later in the same letter defying the demands of convention: "They want me to have form: that means they want me to have their pernicious ossiferous skin-and-grief form, and I won't."[22]

Even before Lawrence came into his own voice fully and confidently—during the rewriting of *The Sisters* as first *The Wedding Ring* and then *The Rainbow* (summer 1913 to spring 1915) and of *The Prussian Officer* stories in the summer of 1914[23]—his writings did not easily fit the schools, conventions, and forms of the writers he was reading. From early on, Lawrence showed a striking independence of artistic imagination, which expressed itself most persistently in the distinctiveness of his techniques. His technique of psychological presentation in *The Rainbow, Women in Love,* and many of the stories is particularly distinctive and remains for many readers more difficult to attune themselves to than the "received experimentalism" of stream of consciousness or interior monologue, which better conforms to our image of ourselves as thinking beings, or as minds in bodies.

What, then, can be said about Lawrence's place in the development of the short story? First, he did read widely in the genre, as is shown by his various references during his early years to Balzac, Gorky, George Eliot, Gissing, Anatole France, Maupassant, Hardy, Chekhov, Gertrude Bone, H. G. Wells, W. W. Jacobs, Anne Douglas Sedgwick, Alphonse Daudet, Zola, and others. But Lawrence expressed interest in or admiration for very different types of writers, reflecting his wide-ranging curiosity and sympathy rather than any intention to imitate slavishly. That Lawrence had little interest in the short story as a genre has been noted by several critics and is reflected in the paucity of his commentary on the genre (brought to light by Cushman's concerted search for it in his essay discussed above). And it seems clear the writers who were most influential on his stories were by and large the same as those who influenced him in prose fiction generally.[24] Important among these was Hardy, from whom Lawrence learned much about natural settings (the "spirit of place"), about the relationships between human personality and the circumambient universe, and about the subtlety and complexity of the forces working subliminally within human beings, and who served Lawrence as sounding board for his own emerging view of life.[25]

Lawrence's influence on subsequent writers is also problematic and has been little discussed. H. E. Bates, in his *The Modern Short Story*, has a chapter entitled "Lawrence and the Writers of Today," in which he argues that "Lawrence, being true to his own vision, will always be closer to life than either Kipling or Wells, and in that respect alone he set an example . . . which a new decade of writers eagerly followed."[26] Elizabeth Bowen, writing in 1947, says, "I believe I could pick up the Lawrence trail across the work of most English novelists making their mark now. Most English of English writers, Lawrence will not be got out of the English bloodstream: he has psychic ancestors, as he must have descendants"—but she does not specify.[27] Philip Hobsbaum is more specific; he points to Lawrence's heightening of demotic speech through metaphor and alliteration "until it almost reaches the level of poetry" as the "aspect of his work that has had so much influence on later writers such as Len Doherty, Alan Sillitoe, Stan Barstow, Stanley Middleton, Bill Naughton, Keith Waterhouse, Philip Callow, among others."[28] Lawrence's influence seems most palpable in the stories of Coppard and Bates (and perhaps T. F. Powys), largely because of similarities of setting and of subject matter. Obviously lacking in even the best stories of these writers, however, are the emotive intensity and the complexity of character that distinguish Lawrence's works.

We can sometimes detect ad hoc evidences of Lawrence's influence on various individual writers or stories, ranging from Hemingway's parody of "The Prussian Officer" in his "An Enquiry," to a more extensive influence on the short stories of Elizabeth Bowen and Aldous Huxley. Because of similarities of theme, situation, and character, many of Huxley's stories invite comparison with Lawrence's—"Hubert and Minnie," for example, recalls Lawrence's stories about temperamentally mismatched lovers, and "The Claxtons" clearly derives from "England, My England." But scrutiny of how Huxley handles these similar elements results in unflattering comparisons: in effect, Huxley's pale, one-dimensional presentation of his characters exposes more starkly the achievement of Lawrence's rich, multidimensional explorations of his characters, demonstrating that Lawrence's distinctive mode of psychological presentation was not a common achievement of his time.

Julian Moynahan has written intelligently on this difficult question of Lawrence's influence on subsequent writers:

> Lawrence's ways of writing a story are not very imitable. Without the animating power of his vision the would-be disciple is apt to produce overblown lyricism, realism run to seed in lushness, hapless parody, or soft-core pornography....
>
> Lawrence had had [*sic*] few close followers... but... his influence has been inescapable and pervasive. He has shown all later writers something fundamental: new forms can be generated through the freeing of feeling, yet this is a process requiring a very arduous discipline, the discipline of utter emotional honesty. (Moynahan, "Foreword" to *A Modern Lover and Other Stories*, [1969], xxii-xxiii; see Part 3, for fuller quotation of Moynahan's remarks.)[29]

Whereas for several decades critics of Joyce have distinguished James Joyce from Stephen Dedalus, even recent Lawrence criticism is infected by tangential biographical questions. Philip Hobsbaum, for example, opens his discussion of Lawrence's late stories with the pronouncement that they "share ... the expression of the author's hatred for certain former friends, notably John Middleton Murry" (Hobsbaum, *Reader's Guide*, 120). Hobsbaum fails to engage the stories because of his critically debilitating assumption that they are flawed by unassimilated animus and rancor. While the autobiographical roots of much of what Lawrence wrote are undeniable, it is a serious mistake to presume that because we know the biographical circumstances behind a story, we therefore know what it is "about," or what attitude Lawrence takes toward the characters or the issues of the work. If we come to Lawrence's works free of such assumptions, we will find in them clear instances of art "transcending" its origins.[30]

Much of the challenge of reading Lawrence's works arises out of his use of narrative point of view, the very aspect of Lawrence's technique Mark Schorer criticizes in "Technique as Discovery." In that essay Schorer judges Lawrence in terms of several assumptions about point of view and literary form that stem from the practice of Henry James, Conrad, and Joyce. The essence of Schorer's criticism is that Lawrence does not remain "objective" in his presentation—that, on the contrary, in *Sons and Lovers*, "Morel and Lawrence are never separated, which is a way of saying that Lawrence maintains for himself in this book the confused attitude of his character." The result, Schorer says, is "a psychological tension which disrupts the form of the novel and obscures its meaning" (Schorer, 76–77).

Lawrence's technique is not, however, a flawed version of the Jamesian method, but an alternative method, in some respects more subtle and more demanding for the reader, that arises from different assumptions about the relation of author to character. Ironically, in illustrating how Lawrence's point of view is muddled, Schorer suggests (only to denigrate) the subtlety Lawrence achieves. "At the same time that *Sons and Lovers* condemns the mother," Schorer writes, "it justifies her." Surely that is no fault; surely Mrs. Morel is so complex a character that she should evoke both condemnation and justification. But since Lawrence does not achieve his complexity of tone through sanctioned modernist techniques, Schorer presumes there is no technique involved. Instead of concluding that the point of view is subtle and complex, he concludes it "is never adequately objectified and sustained" (Schorer, 77).[31]

Lawrence simply did not turn as readily to the literary establishment for his paradigms and standards as did many of his contemporaries, preferring to forge his own modes. One manifestation of his independence is a view of authorial presence significantly different from that being touted by others. The "received" view during the early decades of this century was the ideal of objectivity described by Stephen Dedalus in *A Portrait of the Artist as a Young Man*. According to this view, "the artist, like the God of the creation, remains within or behind or beyond or above his handiwork, invisible, refined out of existence, indifferent, paring his fingernails."[32] But Lawrence had no intention of withdrawing himself from his characters: he aimed rather to dwell in each of them as fully as possible. Thus, while writing from the perspective of a given character, Lawrence strives to put himself fully into the psyche and situation of that character, to empathize with the character sufficiently so as to present vividly and convincingly her feelings, wishes, thoughts—even her confusions. And when he shifts to the perspective of another character, Lawrence does the same for him. Lawrence would, then, believe that good writing aims at balance and fairness in the presentation of character—in the author's keeping his thumb out of the balance—but presumes such balance is best achieved not by distancing oneself from the characters, but by regarding each with as much empathy as possible.

Such aspiration to dwell in his characters does have tangible effects. For one, it renders the tenor of Lawrence's stories utterly different from that of Flaubert's or Maupassant's, so that instead of authorial distance and cool dispassion, there is in every line of Lawrence's prose a quality of energy and intensity. Especially palpable in such early stories as "Odour of Chrysanthemums" and "The Prussian Officer," this energetic quality characterizes most of Lawrence's stories and we feel it strongly even in stories as late as "The Rocking-Horse Winner" and "Sun." For another, this relationship with his characters leaves Lawrence's critics floundering in strange objections. Schorer objects that in *Sons and Lovers* Lawrence "maintains for himself the confused attitude of the character," thus generating "a psychological tension which disrupts the form of the novel and obscures its meaning" (Schorer, 76–77). Ironically, the psychological tension of which Schorer complains is an effect Lawrence must have intended. It could, in fact, be said that Lawrence "presents with wonderful fidelity and complexity the confused attitude of his character," and so generates a "psychological energy that stretches the form of the novel"— and the short story.

The complexity of Lawrence's authorial relationship to his characters arises not only from the various dimensions of personality he is dramatizing, but also from a handling of point of view very different from that of many of his contemporaries. Some of what appears "omniscient" in Lawrence's presentation is by no means authoritative, reflecting instead a character's limited or even mistaken perspective, but presented with such fullness and conviction as to sound authorial. Such material is indeed "authorial" in that it may represent a thought or a feeling or even a somatic state so subliminal or so fleeting that the character has no awareness of it and could not himself give it articulation. Thus the words printed on the page may represent something so subconscious or vaguely formed that the character would deny it to be his thought. Or the text may present with fervor a feeling that is intense but fleeting, that does not represent the character's typical or considered thinking. Or, what is set down on the page may represent a conscious, articulated thought, but one that the character himself does not really believe—a rationalization that allows his true motives or feelings to run on unmolested beneath the surface. And Lawrence may present all such thoughts, feelings, and rationalizations with an energy and vividness that confer apparent authorial sanction. He strives to do justice to a whole array of psychological subtleties that are not often caught in literature and that challenge modernist tabula rasa conceptions of the mind, and he does so with such fidelity to what the character is feeling—not necessarily to what he *understands*—that we must be very careful not to misconstrue it.

If what a character says may indeed be atypical of his true feelings, if comments made by the narrative voice may only *appear* to be authorial, the burden upon the reader is considerable: how can she know where to stand, how does she know how to respond to any given passage? She must, of course, judge by the larger context, and in reading a Lawrence short story, the reader is obliged to remain tentative in responding to any passage, evaluating any character. Only after she has begun to grasp the psychological context of the story and the basic life stances of the characters, can she begin to judge the point of view behind any description or reflection. Reading a Lawrence story involves repeated movements from part to whole and back to part.

The presentation of Isabel's psychology in "The Blind Man" illustrates some of the complexities of Lawrence's use of point of view. Technically, "The Blind Man" is omniscient; the author moves about in time and space and carries us into the minds of the several characters. The story opens with Isabel Pervin waiting for the arrival of her friend Bertie and for the return of her husband. Of her anticipation of Bertie, the reader is told: "Her dearest and oldest friend, a man who seemed almost indispensable to her living, would drive up in the rainy dusk of the closing November day."[33] Isabel's reverie suggests Bertie is important to her in a way simply not borne out by subsequent events, and it is likely that if we could question Isabel as to why she regards Bertie as "indispensable to her living," she would quite honestly deny any such feeling. But Lawrence is not misrepresenting Isabel. In her state of tension and anticipation—rooted deeply in concern for her husband and in her pregnancy, and, more shallowly, in looking forward to both Bertie and Maurice—she truly does have a flicker of feeling that is validly represented by the phrase quoted. In some ways, on some level, she does feel she could hardly stand it if Bertie were not to appear. (Most of us can remember similarly intense feelings of anticipation from our childhood, but adult common sense suppresses and denies such feelings.)

But this impulse in Isabel lies beneath thought and feeling, in some physical dimension not sanctioned by articulation. A level of Isabel's psyche is thus reflected that could not have been penetrated by first-person interior monologue; Isabel would not have said to herself, "My dearest and oldest friend, a man almost indispensable to my living, shall soon drive up." But the use of third-person indirect presentation enables Lawrence to represent states beneath any the character can express, or can even feel very coherently.[34] Such a presentation ventures into psychological terrain almost uncharted and requires great concentration on the part of the reader.

An earlier story, "New Eve and Old Adam," shows a less technically skillful Lawrence seeking ways to dramatize his complex emergent psychological interests.[35] The story is especially interesting because it engages so directly and probes so deeply into the difficult relationship between the husband and wife in a way that very likely draws upon what Lawrence and Frieda had been through in the preceding year— we are told at the outset that the couple "had been married a year" (*LAH*, 161)—but it does so in ways that do not dramatize its material very skillfully or subtly. For example, Lawrence devotes two long paragraphs to describing the husband's feelings as he arrives at the hotel for the night, only to add explicitly, "He was not aware of this." The most interesting, exploratory part of the story occurs when the husband, lying in the dark, is drawn into a liminally-conscious exploration of his wife's perspective on their relationship. It is a strange, daring kind of passage, in that while we are undoubtedly within the husband's psyche, it delves deeply into the wife's feelings about their relationship, evoking her perspective in a way by no means complimentary to him and that seems quite consistent with her feelings as they are presented elsewhere in the story. It seems as if through this experience the husband really does come to feel some of what his wife feels. This passage, and this story as a whole, gives us a tangible sense of what Lawrence meant by his several references during this period to the need for a merging of masculine and feminine perspectives, and his statements that his art was drawing upon Frieda and himself; the process the husband goes through in this story, and that Lawrence had to go through in order to write it, clearly involves a considerable interchange, even merging, of the two perspectives.[36]

But what goes on in the husband's psyche as he lies in the dark is presented too directly, too explicitly. At the outset we are told, "As soon as he had turned out the light, and there was nothing left for his mental consciousness to flourish amongst, it dropped, and it was dark inside him as without" (*LAH*, 172). Some of the subsequent paragraphs involve an interesting but awkward mixture of explicit statement and evocative metaphors, as when Lawrence tells us of the husband's state of being: "But again, the reasonable being in him knew it was ridiculous, and he remained staring at the dark, having the horrible sensation of a roof low down over him; whilst that dark, unknown being, which lived below all his consciousness in the eternal gloom of his blood, heaved and raged blindly against him" (*LAH*, 172). And when these several paragraphs are over, Lawrence says explicitly, "Without knowing it, he suffered that night almost more than he had ever suffered during his life. But it was all below his consciousness" (*LAH*, 173).

This psychologically ambitious story shows how both of these characters are caught up in forces they cannot articulate or gain any real perspective on. In the brief final section of the story, three levels of feeling and motivation are detectable in Lawrence's rendering of the couple's confused relationship. Consider first the wife's charges against the husband: "The unpardonable thing was you told me you loved me.—Your *feelings* have hated me these three months, which did not prevent you from taking my love and every breath from me.—Underneath you undermined me, in some subtle, corrupt way that I did not see because I believed you, when you told me you loved me" (*LAH*, 183).

But the husband is not the villain the wife's statement makes him out, for he understands and controls no better than she the forces with which they are struggling. He *tells* her he loves her, which is true. But on the level just beneath this articulation, his *feelings* (italicized in the story) resent and resist the torture he endures, and he doubtless has

17

been trying to free himself. On a deeper level still than that of coherent feeling, he is committed to his wife in a way that deserves to be called love. But while the presentation does convey their mutual misunderstanding, their confused mixture of need and fear, it lacks the technical skill to explore these subliminal states without frequent resort to explicit statement, and so it only imperfectly dramatizes the complex states of the husband and wife.

In *"A Propos* of *Lady Chatterley's Lover,"* Lawrence observes that everyone has shallow needs and wishes and profound needs and wishes, but that it may be extremely difficult at any given time to discriminate between them (*Phoenix II,* 501). Lawrence allows his characters to reflect both sorts, both levels, of needs and wishes, and the reader cannot easily disentangle them, any more than the character can. In the fine early story "The White Stocking," for example, young Elise does not know precisely what she is after in her flirtation with Sam Adams, but surely it lies in the direction of a fuller, richer relationship with her husband rather than any real involvement with the blustery Adams. And "Two Blue Birds" almost certainly requires a second reading for us to sense that Mrs. Gee's "gallant affairs" mean nothing to her and that she is using them in hopes of stinging her husband into some response.

In his best stories and novels one distinctive feature of Lawrence's work is his ability to represent the psychological states of his characters and their milieu with unparalleled fullness. One of the most interesting essays exploring this topic is Donald Ross's discussion of Lawrence's use of third-person attributed narration. Quoting a paragraph of description-reflection from the wife's point of view in "The Shadow in the Rose Garden," Ross comments,

> These images, the Edenic "gate," the confusion, are not necessarily available to the character's conscious mind. Lawrence does not suggest that she could say in words that these things are her thoughts; in fact, the wife's spoken words are utilitarian and not at all lyrical. In her sparse dialogue, her most expressive words are "strange," "fond," and the cumbersome "not-straightforward." Lawrence uses attributed narration to depict a rich mental life for a virtually inarticulate character.[37]

The only point at which I demur from Ross's analysis is the phrase "mental life," which implies that what Lawrence articulates is present in the wife's *mind*, whereas it involves far more of her psyche and is better described as a *state of being.*

These psychological dimensions of Lawrence's work remain elusive for modernist critics partly because they involve a conception of the self that runs counter to the superficial empiricist/Enlightenment tabula rasa notion that characterizes the modernist frame of mind. Lawrence persistently goes beyond the idea of an "individual mind" to view personality as involving much more than the ego can conceive. For him the self involves an affective penumbra derived from its continuity with the body and with those regions where consciousness shades off into the circumambient physical and cultural milieu.[38] Lawrence's approach to personality recalls Virginia Woolf's description of life as "a luminous halo, a semi-transparent envelope surrounding us from the beginning of consciousness to the end," and in his novels and stories Lawrence tries to convey "this unknown and uncircumscribed spirit."[39]

Lawrence, in his 5 June 1914 letter to Edward Garnett, gives a much-quoted defense of the conception of personality he was attempting to capture in *The Wedding Ring* (later *The Rainbow*):

> I don't agree with you about the Wedding Ring.... I don't think the psychology is wrong: it is only that I have a different attitude to my characters, and that necessitates a different attitude in you, which you are not as yet prepared to give.... [S]omehow—that which is physic—non-human, in humanity, is more interesting to me than the old-fashioned human element—which causes one to conceive a character in a certain moral scheme and make him consistent. The certain moral scheme is what I object to. In Turguenev, and in Tolstoi, and in Dostoievski, the moral scheme into which all the characters fit—and it is nearly the same scheme—is, whatever the extraordinariness of the characters themselves, dull, old, dead.... I don't care so much about what [a] woman *feels*—in the ordinary usage of the word. That presumes an *ego* to feel with. I only care about what the woman *is*—what she *is*—inhumanly, physiologically, materially—according to the use of the word: but for me, what she *is* as a phenomenon (or as representing some greater, inhuman will), instead of what she feels according to the human conception.... You mustn't look in my novel for the old stable ego of the character. There is another ego, according to whose action the individual is unrecognisable, and passes through, as it were, allotropic states which it needs a deeper sense than any we've been

19

used to exercise, to discover are states of the same single radically-unchanged element. (Like as diamond and coal are the same pure element of carbon. The ordinary novel would trace the history of the diamond—but I say "diamond, what! This is carbon." And my diamond might be coal or soot, and my theme is carbon.) (*Letters,* 2:182–84)

Lawrence does not put his ideas here as clearly as he might, struggling as he is with a new conception and against the advice of a respected critic and friend. His point is that the personality, the self, consists of far more than the ego's conception of the self, but that literature has not done justice to those necessarily unformalizable aspects of personality. Lawrence's objection to the practice of the Russians would be clearer if he had not used the word "moral"—a red flag to most present-day critics. What Lawrence is objecting to is these writers' narrow conception of their characters—for the author's conception of a character functions in fiction much as the ego functions in the psychology of an individual, as a conceptual constraint upon the fullness of self. In fiction, especially nineteenth-century fiction, such a conception inevitably has a "moral" aspect, since the character is acting ("rightly" or "wrongly") in a world of other characters. But Lawrence's objection is not to the *morals* of these writers or of their characters, but to the narrowness of their psychological conception.[40]

Confusing too is Lawrence's use of "nonhuman" and "inhuman" when he means "precognitive" or "preindividual." However "generic" Lawrence's conception of his characters is, they are still recognizably human. Lawrence, however, minimizes the "individual" aspects of character, which he believes our age has overemphasized at the expense of deeper elements of the psyche. His professed indifference to what the woman *feels* exemplifies this: he does not wish to confine his presentation to those feelings that are sufficiently clear and coherent to be given sanction by the mind, by articulation. Rather, he strives also to depict "states of being" that are almost physiological rather than mental—for example, Isabel's sense that Bertie is indispensable to her living—but are nevertheless distinctively human. Lawrence is, then, dissatisfied with the "individualism"—that is, the conception of the individual—at the heart of modern literature. He objects to identifying the self with the mind's conception of the self—a tendency he felt was fostered by stream-of-consciousness technique, purporting as it does to present the flow of thought in the mind—and he strives to forge techniques to evoke the self more fully, such as his use of third-person indirect presentation.

One feature of Lawrence's presentation commented on by several critics (and by Lawrence himself in the "Foreword to *Women in Love*") is the evocation of a rhythm, a pulsating quality, that works through the character's psyche. On the page such rhythms are suggested mainly by the repetition of words or images—a technique some critics have found objectionable. But since he wishes to present the psyche more fully, Lawrence must somehow suggest those rhythms, for, as he has said, "[E]very natural crisis in emotion or passion or understanding comes from this pulsing, frictional to-and-fro, which works up to culmination."[41]

Lawrence's complex, multileveled presentation of character is supported and sustained in his works by something that might be called their "psychic texture." This texture reflects a generic psychic milieu in the works, not identifiable with the states of mind of individual characters; it is conveyed through the authorial voice that "contains" the characters and involves a pervasive medium that grows out of setting and event and is more palpably "psychic," in Jung's generic sense of that term, than what is usually meant by mood or atmosphere. The modernist worldview is skeptical of any such element not directly associated with an individual mind; there is in Lawrence's works, however, a quality that is "psychic" and yet cannot be equated with the attitude of any character, or of the narrator. This quality owes a great deal to evocative description of setting and thus to the notion of "spirit of place," but it is by no means limited to physical description: it draws upon the mental and emotional states of individual characters, and it is manifested in the authorial voice even when that voice does not directly reflect the personality of any individual character. This emotional texture, then, provides the medium necessary for Lawrence's sense of individual personality as continuous with environment.[42]

This quality can be illustrated in the opening paragraph of "The Prussian Officer":

> They had marched more than thirty kilometres since dawn, along the white, hot road, where occasional thickets of trees threw a moment of shade, then out into the glare again. On either hand, the valley, wide and shallow, glistened with heat; dark green patches of rye, pale young corn, fallow and meadow and black pine-woods

spread in a dull, hot diagram under a glistening sky. But right in front the mountains ranged across, pale blue and very still, the snow gleaming gently out of the deep atmosphere. And towards the mountains, on and on, the regiment marched between the rye-fields and the meadows, between the scraggy fruit-trees set regularly on either side the highroad. The burnished, dark green rye threw off a suffocating heat, the mountains drew gradually nearer and more distinct. While the feet of the soldiers grew hotter, sweat ran through their hair under their helmets, and their knapsacks could burn no more in contact with their shoulders, but seemed instead to give off a cold, prickly sensation. (*PO*, 1)

This largely "descriptive" passage is presented authorially; it speaks for no individual character. Yet the first word, "They," involves a generic human perspective basic to the tenor of the passage. The heat and glare of the road, the shade of the thickets of trees, have meaning only as they are *experienced* by someone, as do even the contrasts between the fecund crops in the valley and the snow-touched mountains. And this *experienced* dimension of the scene becomes more tangible through the reference to the "suffocating" heat, and in the explicit (but still generic) references to the sensations of "the soldiers" in the last sentence. The description generates an energy, an intensity, a tension (somehow accentuated by the distant but unavailable mountains) that is the appropriate backdrop for the story.

The brief second paragraph, beginning "He" rather than "They," is so continuous with the first that the individual referred to is easily absorbed into the milieu, almost as if the first paragraph had expressed his sense of things: "He walked on and on in silence, staring at the mountains ahead, that rose sheer out of the land, and stood fold behind fold, half earth, half heaven, the heaven, the barrier with slits of soft snow in the pale, bluish peaks" (*PO*, 1). The milieu thus established acts as a kind of psychic equivalent of the all-pervasive electromagnetic field and in this story in particular contributes a great deal to the distinctive energy of the work.

Modernist critics, skeptical of the existence of an affective dimension that is not the expression of an individual mind, might be tempted to attribute these affects to the authorial "persona," but of course no such Jamesean entity appears in this story. It is more in tune with what Lawrence is presenting here to regard this affective dimension as a public affective aura, manifesting itself most distinctively in human persons, but stemming from the terrain, from the heat and humidity of the day, as well as from the group experience of these soldiers on this march. To deny this dimension, or to regard it as sheerly individual, renders us unresponsive to a characteristic, essential aspect of Lawrence's work.

Another insufficiently recognized and understood dimension of Lawrence's work is its "contextuality," its scrupulous fidelity to and simulation of the immediate situation of the characters. Lawrence's contextual integrity, his evocation of a full, detailed psychological context for his characters, involves him in a fidelity to the characters' situation that many readers are not prepared to credit, largely because of the assumption that Lawrence manipulates characters in order to illustrate some aspect of his "doctrine." On the contrary, Lawrence strives in his fiction to do justice to the full complexity of the living situation he is depicting, and he often succeeds so well as to transcend any didactic "point." Contextuality is integral to the exploratory aim of Lawrence's art, in that a true and subtle exploration can occur only if a character's situation is rendered with regard for all the strains, uncertainties, and ambiguities involved.

A proper regard for the rigorous contextuality of Lawrence's works means that in order to understand why one of Lawrence's characters thinks or acts as she does, the reader should refer first not to the social class the character "represents," nor to the traits of her biographical "original," nor to the Lawrencean doctrine she presumably embodies. He should refer first to the character's psychological *context* within the story, with all its stresses, fears, enticements to role-playing or to evasion, and so on. Only if the reader has sufficient faith in the subtlety of Lawrence's art that he is willing to re-create in his own mind the situation of the character will he grasp the forces working upon that character and see why she reacts as she does. Further, Lawrence's precisely adjusted contextuality means that each situation is necessarily different, and a character's needs or responses in one particular situation should not be generalized into a Lawrencean rule of conduct. For example, many of Lawrence's stories depict a crisis a character must respond to either through self-assertion or self-effacement. But simply because self-assertion is the appropriate response for one character in one situation, we should not infer that Lawrence advocates self-assertion, or even that this character should always act assertively.[43]

As we shall see, only in the light of the full context of the situation of "England, My England" can we understand why Egbert has moved so far down the road of self-disavowal and apparent irresponsibility—

qualities cultivated in him by the particular circumstances and events the story depicts. Also, the ending of "Odour of Chrysanthemums" provides another subtle example of Lawrence's contextuality at work, and at the same time illustrates the divergence of his mode of psychological presentation from the rather simplistic "epiphanic" revelation that characterizes many modernist stories.

The complexity of Lawrence's relationship with his characters is compounded by the kinds of judgments his works make about them. Presuming that Lawrence's stories intend to inculcate some doctrine or to express some personal pique, critics often seek to distinguish heroes from villains according to whether the characters represent Lawrence and his ideas. But this is a false, superficial criterion. Lawrence does "judge" his characters—that is, he does evoke from us an evaluation of them—but his characters are judged primarily on whether they are life-affirmers or life-deniers.

The most important question to ask about a character in Lawrence's works is whether she is trying, however imperfectly, to open herself to life, to run the risk of engaging the new, to have faith that the present life crisis can be broken through into some new direction; or whether she is trying to protect or insulate herself against life, trying defensively to maintain some status quo she fears represents the best, or the safest, that she can ever achieve. This, rather than their manifestation of any Lawrencean idea, is the criterion by which we are to judge, to evaluate, Lawrence's characters: are they trying to remain responsive to the new demands that experience makes on them, or are they trying simply to protect themselves against life and change?

As straightforward as this criterion may seem, in the contexts evoked in the works it becomes quite complex. The character who would be a life-affirmer must on occasion act "negatively"—that is, must break off a relationship or go through a phase of retrogression or withdrawal; the life-denier, on the other hand, may be subtle in her evasions of novelty—so subtle as to turn to sexual passion or to the clichés of Christian charity as a means of escape from what she lacks the courage to face. Nor is any single act likely to reveal the character's true attitude toward life; for that, the larger context of the story is required.

Furthermore, our "evaluation" of a character in these terms must be distinguished from the attitude we may take toward her: even if we judge a character to be making a wrong decision about her life—a life-denying decision—we may yet sympathize with her in her failure. For example, the more we come to understand Egbert in "England, My England," the more clearly do some of his acts appear to be wrong, but the more too we come to sympathize with him, to wish we could help him avoid a mistaken, self-destructive life course. After the accident to Joyce, Egbert entirely sells out his own earlier best qualities. We are told that "when the war broke out his whole instinct was against it: against war" (*EME*, 27), and yet he seizes upon the opportunity war provides to bring his negation to a culmination. Egbert's progressive devolution into fatalism and despair, so terribly reflected in the details of his death, evokes the reader's sympathy, and yet Egbert must be judged to have made a life mistake in surrendering to his own dissolution.

One thrust of the preceding pages has been to argue against using Lawrence's "doctrines" as a crutch in approaching his stories. But none of these adjurations denies that Lawrence's works can and should be read in conjunction with the ideas he proposes more directly in his essays, reviews, and letters. Two points must be emphasized: first, such ideas should be called into play only after some basic sense of the story as story has been arrived at; second, the story will always involve some "special case," some variation on the more explicitly stated idea. For example, having come to some understanding of the human relationships between the officer and the orderly in "The Prussian Officer," the reader may then approach these characters in terms of the categories of mental consciousness and blood consciousness. But insofar as the orderly "represents" the blood consciousness, his mechanical, reflexive response to the life challenge presented by the officer, and his subsequent collapse and death, hint strongly of limitations in that mode of consciousness. Surely the young orderly had a great deal to live for, and surely it would have been better had he been able to summon up the cunning or the understanding to elude the officer's challenge before it reached life-destroying proportions. But, limited creature that he is, the orderly cannot do this, and so he dies almost as an animal would in response to an attack—not a very pointed illustration of Lawrence's presumed belief in the superiority of the blood consciousness.

Attention to point of view, contextuality, and evaluative judgment is necessary in order to appreciate Lawrence's subtle, distinctive modes of presentation. Too schematic an approach to his works inevitably fails to do them justice, especially if the point of view through which the story is presented embodies the character's own confusions and evasions. So subtle can this contextuality become that Lawrence may depict a character who is basically a life-affirmer but who is so confused by the life crisis he is facing (as one is always confused in a true crisis), that he makes a wrong—that is, a life-denying—move, but the reader must be sufficiently attuned to the larger context of the story to understand and sympathize with what is happening.

Whatever perils such subtle contextuality may involve for the reader, whatever opportunity for misreading, it is nonetheless necessary to Lawrence's deepest artistic purposes that he depict his characters' situations in their fullest complexity. How realistic, and how worthwhile, would it be for Lawrence to purport to depict a crisis and yet to show the characters caught up in it acting in perfectly clear-minded fashion? It is precisely this audacious subtlety, this fidelity to experience, that is so valuable in Lawrence's art and makes his short stories so distinctive and rewarding. To abort these qualities by forcing preconceptions upon the stories is to destroy what is finest in them and to deprive us of both pleasure and insight.

Before turning to interpretations of individual stories, I want to touch briefly on three other points in regard to reading Lawrence's stories: his gift for deft evocation of the fictive situation, the need for an inferential leap in reading some of the stories, and the important differences among recurrent situations and types in the stories.

Another of Lawrence's great gifts as a writer—one more obvious in the stories than in the novels—is his ability to establish deftly the essentials of his fictive situation. In just a few sentences he can sketch for us the fundamentals of a character's situation—things the character himself cannot realize. Other great short story writers demonstrate a similar intuition as to which details are appropriate and evocative, which details will serve to bring the scene to life and draw the reader's imagination into active play. This quality is obvious in the openings of some of Joyce's *Dubliners* stories and in several of Hemingway's stories. (Hemingway commented that the reader can be relied on to supply a great deal if the writer has done his job well.) These writers begin their stories having evoked the characters' situation and physical milieu very precisely, and having implicated the reader in the process from the outset.

Lawrence has this same gift in the less tangible sphere of his characters' psychological and spiritual situations. He can deftly convey to us things about the character's relationships to others closest to him, to his circumambient universe, even to himself, that the character has no awareness of and that provide just the right narrative and psychological point of departure for the story.

The characters' "psychic situation" is necessarily less tangible and thus harder to "imagize" than the physical milieu, involving as it does a subtle characterization of exactly where the character stands in the sympathetic/voluntaristic ebb and flow of feelings that subsist between him and those persons and things and events closest to him. To say simply that a couple is married tells us nothing as to whether they are presently in or out of phase with one another, or about how their "being married" is currently affected by the dozens of other relationships in which they are enmeshed. Our psychological and spiritual situation at any given time is far more complex and subtle than our physical one, yet since it is less tangible we appreciate less readily this gift for precise evocation of psychic context that is so distinctive a part of Lawrence's fictional technique.[44]

While this technique is more overt in Lawrence's later, fabulistic stories, it is a feature of his fiction from early on. If Lawrence "learned" this from anyone, it may have been from Chekhov, whose stories often have a brevity that conceals their psychological depth, because he so easily establishes the essential situation—though some of Hawthorne's "parables" (as Lawrence called them in *Studies in Classic American Literature*, 152) have this same quality of exposition.

There is, however, one caveat: in Lawrence this technique can function deceptively, in that what appears to be a deft authorial fixing of coordinates may turn out to be a character's own less-than-reliable judgment about himself, cast in language that appears authoritative. Once again, the reader must remain tentative in engaging the story, relying always upon the larger context to clarify the status, the authority, of such broad strokes of characterization.

Partly because of Lawrence's skill in establishing the situations of his characters, partly because of his concern for "contextuality," partly because of his beginning many of his stories in medias res, reading a Lawrence short story sometimes requires an inferential leap, an heuristic assumption, in order to discover an Archimedean point from which the story can be approached. The best perspective for viewing the story may be discovered only when we make some hardly justified inferential leap, and then reread the story from the perspective of that position. Once we have found a valid perspective, the various elements of the story will fall into place as they have not done before.

Something similar is necessary in some of Hemingway's stories, where his minimalist understatement and implicitness require us to infer certain things about the characters' situation if we are ever to see what is going on in the story. In Hemingway's stories, what we must infer often seems to be expository information, and we feel that his provision of more facts could supply the lack. But in Lawrence what we must infer is not information but a matter of attitude and of perspective. It involves implicit aspects of the characters' personalities and situations that mere factual exposition would not clarify. The striking capacity of Lawrence's stories to reverse themselves on us, causing us suddenly to glimpse a character or situation in an utterly different light, almost like one of those diagrams illustrating perceptual shifts of figure and ground (Is it a vase, or opposing profiles?) shows the necessity of our making some inferential leap. This is not to claim a single "valid" perspective from which to view a story, but rather to say that finding a certain perspective from which to view the story can have great clarifying power. I would never rule out the possibility that my next rereading of any of these stories might reveal some other even richer or more fruitful perspective.

Interpreting a story by Lawrence, then, is not simply a matter of detailed psychological scrutiny and explication of passages, but of positing a perspective from which the story is to be seen, a perspective often inferred from implicit elements of the situation and arrived at only after repeated trials and adjustments, and re-reading the story from the new perspective, so as to sense its appropriateness. The difficulty we often experience in finding just the right perspective on Lawrence's stories results not from obscurantism on his part, but from the subtle balance and finely exploratory quality of his writing. This balance manifests itself in our difficulty in discovering whose story we are reading—that is, from whose perspective the events deserve to be seen.

My readings of several of the stories involve heuristic assumptions and inferences about the characters' situations that may not seem sanctioned by the text. But some such inferential moves are necessary as a *point d'appui* for reading many of them. Our willingness as readers to be inferential and speculative is the counterpart of Lawrence's exploratory mode of writing. Without such venturesomeness on our own part, we may never gain access to the richness of the story.

It is of course helpful and clarifying to recognize recurrent types and situations in D. H. Lawrence's works: the refined and withdrawn male observer-character; the coal miner and his more educated wife; the aggressive male who would put the woman's spirit to sleep; the woman laying out her husband's body, and so on. But we should never presume an identity among such characters or situations from work to work. On the contrary, we should recognize that Lawrence is almost always playing variations on a situation or type, and so we must be especially alert to the subtle differences among them.

Lawrence expresses his sense of human potentiality by exploring situations of great meaning or interest to him from different angles, or in terms of various contingencies of character or situation. He returns to the situation of the collier with a sophisticated wife to see how their relationship might work out differently if she were more empathetic or forgiving, or if the collier were more self-secure and less defensive, or if either of them could glimpse the perspective of the other. Or, considering a tenuous relationship between a young man and woman, he may explore the effects of different degrees of aggressive "masculinity" on the part of the young male (see "The Fox," "You Touched Me," and "The Shadow in the Rose Garden"). While we should then be alert for recurrent situations and types within Lawrence's works, we should be even more attentive to the differences among them, and the very different end-points these differences can lead to.

"Odour of Chrysanthemums"

"Odour of Chrysanthemums," especially in its conclusion, provides a subtle example of Lawrence's "contextuality," and at the same time illustrates how his mode of psychological presentation diverges from the rather simplistic "epiphanic" revelation that characterizes so many modernist stories. Critics of "Odour of Chrysanthemums" have made much of Elizabeth's presumed "revelation" dramatized in the story's closing pages: her "realization" of how little she and her husband, Walter, have impinged on one another's lives, of their essential isolation from one another.[45] Many of these critics assume that this realization is virtually epiphanic, that is, that Elizabeth understands fully and clearly what the import of this experience is.[46]

But I propose another perspective, one growing out of my profound respect for the story's contextuality. In my view, the thrust of the story is not so simply cognitive; the "point" of the story is not simply a "realization" on Elizabeth's part, or a "truth" about human experi-

29

ence that Lawrence himself has discovered. Rather, Lawrence's aim in this story is to explore and faithfully represent Elizabeth's complex, distinctive reactions to this trauma—of which the "realization" about her husband and herself is only one not totally reliable part.

I argued earlier that Lawrence's writing is distinctively exploratory, that in his writing he works through experiences he found especially meaningful or troubling. Nowhere is that exploratory quality clearer than in his works that focus on the psychological and spiritual states of coal miners and their wives, a situation of great personal importance to the author. He returns again and again to a coal miner and his wife, in *Sons and Lovers*, in *The Widowing of Mrs. Holroyd*, in "Nottingham and the Mining Countryside," and in many of the early short stories. A special facet of that motif is scrutinized in the endings of successive drafts of this short story.

That the scene of the wife (or mother) of a dead miner engaged in caring for his laid-out body had a special meaning for Lawrence is obvious; several such scenes in his works have been discussed in detail by Keith Cushman (*Lawrence at Work*, chap. 3). Cushman addresses not only the various drafts of this story, but other related passages as well—including *The White Peacock*, part 1, chapter 4 (in which Cyril and his mother view the corpse of his father), the ending of *Mrs. Holroyd*, and chapter 9 of *The Rainbow* (where the body of the drowned Tom Brangwen is attended to).

We know from biographical evidence that Lawrence struggled with this scene in his successive revisions of the story.[47] Keith Cushman shows convincingly that the changes in the ending even at the last stages of composition were radical and significant, and he construes these changes in terms of Lawrence's recognition of a fundamental life insight—namely, the fact of human isolation, even experienced by those who have long been married. Cushman says, "In later versions of the story, the experience of seeing and washing her husband's beautiful body as it lies in the repose of death is a powerful epiphany, a shattering but illuminating experience that for the first time reveals to her the nature of her marriage" (*Lawrence at Work*, 57–58). Cushman further notes that for Lawrence "even in the most intimate relationship there is always an unbridgeable gulf. It is at this time that this basic assumption underlying his work throughout the remainder of his career emerged in its mature form." Shortly thereafter he says that the scene "has now become a lesson in human isolation" (*Lawrence at Work*, 68, 69).[48]

This claim that the story involves a lesson or truth Lawrence (or Elizabeth) had finally come to see is by no means unique to Cushman. Mara Kalnins speaks of "Elizabeth's recognition of her failure" and of the "shock of revelation" (*Critical Essays*, 151), and J. C. F. Littlewood says that in rewriting the ending, Lawrence "discovered the meaning that had always been waiting to be found in the story" ("Lawrence's Early Tales," 123). But to state the story's purpose in terms of such an abstract, universal truth about human nature demeans the particular situation of the story and makes the distinctive personalities of the characters virtually irrelevant. And Littlewood's claim involves a hypostatization of "meaning" that is troubling and seems inconsistent with Lawrence's view of art as something that eschews absolutes.

What Lawrence wrestled with in his successive revisions of the story was not the philosophical/ideational challenge of what that situation means, but the exploratory/artistic challenge of how to be faithful to the powerful and complex emotional structure of such an experience as it unfolds for the character. Lawrence knew that few experiences are more powerful and more traumatic than attending to the dead but beautifully intact body of someone you have loved and lived with for many years, especially if the relationship has been marked by strong clashes of will and personality. And one part of the challenge of being faithful to the emotions stimulated by this dramatic situation is to do justice to precisely this tendency on the part of the survivor—especially one so self-reliant as Elizabeth Bates—to deal with the experience by gleaning from it some "understanding," regardless of how well or poorly that understanding matches what she had lived through. Elizabeth Bates is just the sort of person who badly needs to retain control of herself and her emotions, and who would try to achieve such control through coming to some conclusion about it.

I am, then, skeptical about the claim that the heart of this much-rewritten story is a "meaning" or a "truth" Lawrence or his character discovers. It is simplistic and contrary to my sense of Lawrence's view of complex human relations that Elizabeth Bates could, within an hour of her husband's death, have come to such a clear and valid understanding of the event that these critics claim for her. And Cushman himself makes one comment that suggests the unlikelihood of such an outcome. "The passionate, onrushing prose of the last pages of the story perfectly captures the inner experience of the stunned wife as, almost instantly, she is forced for the first time to come to grips with what her life has been" (*Lawrence at Work*, 71).[49] I do not see how the prose can simultaneously be faithful to the inner experience of the stunned wife *and* present her as coming so quickly to a clear, valid "understanding" of the death of her husband and the meaning of their relationship. Such instantaneous epiphanic revelations are more in keeping with the view of human nature we find in Maupassant or O. Henry. Lawrence's works testify to how impossible it is for us to come to any cognitive understanding of our immediate experience, and to show how prone, and how skillful, we are at using self-deceiving ploys to evade any powerful, novel experience.[50]

Those critics who regard the story as providing a revelation typically focus almost exclusively on its last few pages. While Lawrence worked that section over repeatedly and carefully, we cannot simply disregard the first half of the story. The beginning offers an extended presentation of the personality of Elizabeth, as well as her relationships with her father, her neighbors, and her children, and thereby provides a necessary context for understanding Elizabeth's reactions at story's end, showing that she and Walter have impinged upon one another's lives in a variety of ways.

If the purpose of the story were to convey the abstract life-truth that we are all inescapably isolated from one another, it would matter little whether Elizabeth is "a tall woman of imperious mien, handsome, with definite black eyebrows," whose black hair is parted exactly and whose mouth is closed with disillusionment (*PO*, 182), or a dumpy, disheveled woman who loves gossiping with the neighbors. But surely the "point" of this story is a function of the distinctive character who dominates it. Elizabeth is not simply a generic "miner's wife"; she is the sort of person who very much values control and self-possession and self-reliance—doubtless her past disappointments with Walter have made her value these qualities all the more. It is characteristic of her that even at this time of terrible trauma—or perhaps *especially* at this time of soul-shaking emotions—she must do everything she can to maintain control. This striving for control is expressed in a variety of ways, from her obvious suppression of her own emotions in regard to what is happening, to her pressing upon herself the need to protect her children, to her attempt to lay claim to Walter, to her need to comprehend the situation, to glean some life-insight out of the experience.

When she first learns of Walter's death, Elizabeth is mainly concerned to stay in control emotionally and mentally. She devotes herself to the necessary preparations for receiving his body; she quiets and consoles his mother; she protects the children from the scene. But when she tries to lay claim to her husband's body in a way comparable to how she had laid claim to his spirit during life, we are told, "Elizabeth felt countermanded. She saw him, how utterly inviolable he lay in himself. She had nothing to do with him. She could not accept it" (*PO*, 196). But even embracing the body does not enable any connection; she feels "driven away," feels he is "impregnable" (*PO*, 196).

Rebuffed in these attempts finally to lay claim to her husband, Elizabeth expresses her frustration by swinging to the opposite pole and telling herself they had never impinged on one another in any meaningful way: "There had been nothing between them . . . she knew she had never seen him, and he had never seen her, they had met in the dark and fought in the dark, not knowing whom they met nor whom they fought. And now she saw, and turned silent in the seeing. For she had been wrong. She had said he was something he was not; she had felt familiar with him. Whereas he was apart all the while, living as she never lived, feeling as she never felt" (*PO*, 198). While this reaction on her part is natural and understandable, its fidelity to what had passed between them during their life together is highly doubtful.

There is a similar neatness and simplicity to her presumptuous claim that this dead man had nothing to do with the children (*PO*, 198). This claim is in fact contradicted by earlier passages of the story, where we are told, "As the mother watched her son's sullen little struggle with the wood, she saw herself in his silence and pertinacity, she saw the father in her child's indifference to all but himself" (*PO*, 184). But later, in her strong reaction, Elizabeth explicitly denies this reality, saying, "There were the children—but the children belonged to life. This dead man had nothing to do with them. He and she were only channels through which life had flowed to issue in the children" (*PO*, 198). As a "truth" about life, this sounds more like rationalization or self-delusion, and seems better explained as a part of the strong sense of denial and isolation Elizabeth is putting herself through in the midst of this trauma. It is interesting as well that Lawrence (who could have done something quite different) presents Elizabeth as pregnant, in contrast to Walter whom she regards as "impregnable" (*PO*, 196). But Elizabeth is forced by her present mood to deny this child, to regard it not as the locus of new hopes and possibilities, but as "a weight apart from her" (*PO*, 197), and "like ice in her womb" (*PO*, 198). Perhaps most simplistic of all is her judgment that "She saw this episode of her life closed" (*PO*, 198). She may wish this to be true, may even strive to make it true, and in her present state she no doubt finds the idea consoling, but this "insight" will not likely remain intact through the next several weeks and months, while she carries and gives birth to their child.

Among the most revealing of Elizabeth's reactions is her self-castigation for having denied Walter, followed by her consequent exaggeration of how cruelly she had injured this man and how clearly she now sees her fault. Such a moral/emotional swing on her part seems wonderfully faithful to how a woman of her temperament would respond to such an experience. Furthermore, she can afford so categorical a view of her husband and their situation only because Walter is dead. It is much easier for her to tell herself in relationship to a dead man that "she denied him what he was—she saw it now. She had refused him as himself," than it would be to come to terms with the living, willful, and inscrutable man. And so it is too neat—and ultimately incorrect—to say that death has "restored the truth": quite the contrary, death has allowed Elizabeth to indulge in a simplification that life would never have permitted.[51]

But Elizabeth should not be judged harshly, for some such simplification of her relation with Walter is precisely what is needed, indeed is almost inevitable, for someone in her situation; given her context of loss and shock, it is something we might expect from her. Is the first reaction after a shock of bereavement likely to be the "true" one? Is it not more likely to be colored by confusion, by deep fear, by guilt, and by the need to find some simple conception of things to hold onto? This is where the real center of interest is for Lawrence in this situation, not in some O. Henryesque "realization," the simplicity of which demeans their relationship.

Other aspects of the story should suggest to us the partiality, the incompleteness, of Elizabeth's reaction to the death of her husband—for example, the contrast between her reaction and that of Walter's mother. The mother's reaction is "simpler" in several respects—more immediately emotional, less guarded—and is included in the story mainly as a clarifying foil to Elizabeth's more complex reaction. Their reactions differ most in that the older woman's is more spontaneous and emotional, in contrast to Elizabeth's, whose temperament demands reserve and denial of feeling. But interestingly, we are told that when "the old woman wailed aloud . . . this relieved Elizabeth" (*PO*, 193), though her immediate explicit reaction is to object to the old woman's noise while playing her role of protector of the children.

The mother's response also gives us a view of Walter we can contrast with that held by Elizabeth—a view of a young man who was "a happy lad at home" (*PO*, 192), one capable of hearty laughter (*PO*, 197). Even when their response to the dead men is similar, it serves to clarify something about Elizabeth's reaction: the mother's obviously romantic view of Walter as a lad should suggest to us the correspondingly selective, incomplete nature of Elizabeth's view of the dead man.

Any artist who depicts a character involved in a powerful life situation necessarily feels some tension between his artistic wish to be faithful to the character's experience, and his wish to emerge from the presentation with some coherent gist or point. This dilemma becomes all the more challenging if the situation involves powerful emotions for the writer himself, if he is projecting the type of character who feels a distinctive need for ideational understanding and control. This is the dilemma and challenge Lawrence faced in writing this scene.

What Lawrence achieved in the "final" *Prussian Officer* version of the story was not primarily an insight for himself or Elizabeth, but something very different, and artistically far more valuable. He achieved the capacity to keep his thumb out of the ideational, thematic balance—an artistic "negative capability," by virtue of which he can let his characters realize themselves so fully that he can explore their responses to the most emotionally charged experiences without any fretful searching after truth. Keith Cushman makes one comment that tends in this same direction. Of this story that we know was rooted so deeply in Lawrence's own situation, he says, "A scholar lacking the biographical background of 'Odour of Chrysanthemums' would be hard pressed to discover the author's deep personal involvement in its materials" (*Lawrence at Work*, 47). This means that in regard to this very personal, charged material, Lawrence has achieved an artistic distance that enables the story—and its characters—to have a life of its own.

"The Shadow in the Rose Garden"

"The Shadow in the Rose Garden" is one of several stories from the *Prussian Officer* volume that has been discussed in terms of how its revisions reflect Lawrence's artistic growth.[52] The three versions of the story do illustrate Lawrence's increasing psychological insight and his growing control over techniques that sound the depths of his characters' psyches. The successive versions also show him exploring a courtship/marriage situation from different angles and perspectives, so while the version published in the *Prussian Officer* volume is Lawrence's last one, it should not be regarded as "definitive." Other short story writers have testified that their stories are so much of one piece that the end is virtually contained within the beginning.[53] But Lawrence's frequent reworking of his stories shows this not to be the case with him; rather, he often uses his stories to explore the several possibilities latent in a situation, given a different turn of events or different proclivities within the characters.

The *Prussian Officer* version of the story turns on the wife's ambivalent feelings about her past engagement and her present marriage. But the psychological focus of the story—the exact nature of the wife's problem—is elusive, mainly because the story so subtly reflects the woman's own complex, confused perspective. At first glance the story may appear to be about a mismatch between a sensitive woman and a socially inferior, defensive, and somewhat coarse husband, but that interpretation would be to accept too readily the most superficial level of the wife's perspective. On further scrutiny, it appears the woman is held in thrall by her romantic memory of a past love relationship, a memory that prevents her from living in the present, loving her husband, and accepting their marriage.

Viewed in this way, the story seems to rework a familiar Lawrencean pattern: A woman who sees herself as refined and idealistic is fixated on a past love relationship that for some reason failed, but she still regards it nostalgically, idealistically. More recently she has paired herself with a man she claims to regard as beneath herself; the choice of this man is her own, though she may feel him to have been forced upon her by circumstances. We sense she has chosen him for more positive reasons than she realizes. She finds herself incapable, however, of exorcising the old romantic image and giving herself wholeheartedly to the present less-than-perfect situation.

But "The Shadow in the Rose Garden" is complicated by the fact that the woman seems to be so fully aware of this scenario and seems even to be *telling it to herself*, and there are hints of another layer beneath the surface. It may well be that the collapse of her earlier "engagement" to the vicar's son is not the *cause* of her present problems, but an earlier instance of her persistent tendency toward self-protection and life denial. This possibility is raised by the wife's sense that she is self-imprisoned and wants to be freed from self-imposed constraints. If so, then this is not simply the story of a sensitive woman traumatized by a past loss, but rather a portrait of a woman struggling against a deeper-rooted fear of giving herself unqualifiedly to relationships. As we shall see, evidence does indicate that she is fearful of giving herself in any relationship, that she uses various devices to preserve the safety of her position, and that she believes herself to prefer some state of ethereal dissolution to the tangible commitments of a relationship.

"The Shadow in the Rose Garden" is a story of considerable subtlety. It paints a finely shaded portrait of a young woman sufficiently self-possessed to manipulate those around her, especially her accommodating husband, Frank, but who is unable or unwilling to shake off the dead past and live in the present. For whatever reasons, the woman has never fully committed herself to her marriage, and she holds her husband at bay. Her view of the situation seems to be that memories of her past "engagement" constitute a stumbling block to her getting on with her life, the justification for her present reserve. Her earlier failed engagement thus serves as an excuse for maintaining a distance between herself and her husband that keeps him insecure and "suppressed," and that prevents their relationship from achieving depth and richness.

These same qualities of defensiveness and reserve on the woman's part may well have brought about the failure of her earlier relationship with the vicar's son. We know relatively little about that relationship, but what we do know suggests problems between them. Significantly, that relationship, which seems never to have become an "engagement," failed not because of the death of her young man, but because he inexplicably and precipitately left her to go to war. The details of the courtship are vague, and all of them are revealed through the young woman. We are told, "We were as good as engaged for nearly a year, though nobody knew—at least—they talked—but—it wasn't open. Then he went away—" (*PO*, 131). That their relationship was kept secret and their engagement never formalized suggests hesitation and reluctance on someone's part. Of his departure she says simply, "Then ... he suddenly went out to fight in Africa" (*PO*, 131). Earlier we were told that he was "an officer—a sub-lieutenant," and that after a quarrel with his colonel he "came out of the army" (*PO*, 130). It seems unlikely, then, that he was conscripted, and so we must wonder why a young man who was "as good as engaged" would "suddenly" decide to go off to fight in Africa. Did the same reserve,

diffidence, and manipulativeness that have so frustrated and suppressed the husband cause the vicar's son to turn from her to the more
tangible and straightforward challenges of the war? Perhaps she was
reluctant to commit herself to a man so strong and willful as to argue
with his superior officer, and he, frustrated in the limbo of their relationship, went back to the army and the war.

The story achieves a deft and detailed portrait of the woman, showing her to have an aloof manner and yet be adept at maintaining subtle
psychological control. Though she is described as "abstracted" and
with "her face yearning" (*PO*, 121), she is not passive, and the story
shows her using subtle manipulations to keep Frank off balance and
insecure. Furthermore, the decision to visit this village is hers, not his,
and on this morning they go into the garden of their cottage at her suggestion (*PO*, 122). And she uses her wiles—her "winning smile" and
"pretty wilfulness" (*PO*, 124)—with the gardener as well as with her
husband.

While the woman is the focal character, the story opens with a presentation of her husband. Even though Frank has no inkling of what
will later happen, he exists in a "state of self-suppression" (*PO*, 121)
that is not new to him and is reflected in certain details of his experience. Of the several paintings on the wall, the one he gives "careful
but hostile attention to" is "The Stag at Bay," and when he tries the
lid of the piano, he finds it locked (*PO*, 121). Catching sight of his wife
at the window, "It irked [him] that she should continue abstracted
and in ignorance of him" (*PO*, 121), and we sense this feeling of being
ignored and suppressed is common with him.

A passage later in the story subtly reveals Frank's sense of their relationship and the source of the suppression he so persistently feels.
After his wife returns, "no more sensible to him than if he did not exist" (*PO*, 128), we are told,

> All his suppressed anger against her who held herself superior to
> him filled and blackened his heart. Though he had not known it,
> yet he had never really won her, she had never loved him. She had
> taken him on sufferance. This had foiled him. He was only a labor-
> ing electrician in the mine, she was superior to him. He had always
> given way to her. But all the while the injury and ignominy had
> been working in his soul because she did not hold him seriously.
> (*PO*, 129)

This passage is a subtle example of Lawrence's "authorial" presentation of the inner state of a character. While the phrase "Though he had not known it" sounds firmly authorial, subsequent statements quickly take on Frank's own perspective. The sentence "He was only a laboring electrician in the mine, she was superior to him," reflects not the truth about their relationship, but Frank's view of it, doubtless inferred from many hints from his wife. Even the phrase "she had never really loved him," occurring in the same sentence as the authorial opening, I take not to be a statement of the truth, but the surfacing of a threat that has existed as a subcurrent in their marriage. There is, then, some exaggeration and distortion here in regard to his inferiority to her and her not really loving him, typical of what we often find when Lawrence presents the psyches of characters in crisis. But this passage clearly reveals the husband's insecure, defensive position. This sense of his inferiority is one of the devices the wife has used over the years to exercise control of the relationship.

Frank is not, however, an utterly passive or defeated character. When he catches a glimpse of himself in the mirror we are told, "His figure was rather small, but alert and vigorous," and that his look of "self-commiseration" mingles with "his appreciation of his own physiognomy" (*PO,* 121). When they walk out into the garden together, he is described as "walking in an easy, confident fashion" (*PO,* 122).

The couple met three or four years earlier and has presumably been married for much of that time.[54] Given the generally self-possessed, even manipulative, nature of the woman, it is unlikely she was forced into the marriage; her husband is probably a man of her own choosing, though their relationship may have begun when she was on the rebound from the departure of her previous lover. The landlady's judgment concerning the couple is worth taking note of: "Just of a height they are. She wouldn't ha' married a man less than herself in stature, I think, though he's not her equal otherwise" (*PO,* 122). Whether the landlady is a model of perspicacity we cannot know, but her observation exists in the story for some purpose. Her judgment suggests the woman has carefully chosen the man she has married—one whom she does not utterly look down on, but can control.

The woman's personality is the central interest, the central enigma, of the story. We learn a great deal about her from her sojourn in the rose garden. Her time alone in the garden before the vicar's son appears suggests she regards the garden and what it evokes as a retreat from reality, a retreat even from the burdens of selfhood. Wearing a hat adorned with roses (*PO*, 124), she wanders through the rose garden "in abstraction," "lingering, like one who has gone back into the past" (*PO*, 125). Then she pauses to wonder narcissistically over a white rose "that was greenish, like ice, in the centre" (*PO*, 125), and finally she takes her seat among the white roses and tries utterly to efface herself: "She sat quite still, feeling her own existence lapse. She was no more than a rose, a rose that could not quite come into blossom, but remained tense" (*PO*, 126). This sense of herself as a rose not capable of blossom, and of her own tension, hints of something in her situation she herself would like to be free of.[55]

It is noteworthy that this spell is shattered not by her recognition of her old lover, but by the mere presence in her garden of another: the "shadow" of the story's title is cast over her retreat *before* the person who casts it is recognized:

> Then she started cruelly as a shadow crossed her and a figure moved into her sight. It was a man who had come in slippers unheard. He wore a linen coat. The morning was shattered, the spell vanished away. She was only afraid of being questioned. He came forward. She rose. Then, seeing him, the strength went from her and she sank on the seat again. (*PO*, 126)

The woman is of course shocked by seeing the lunatic shell of her former lover, but her subsequent reaction suggests she is more deeply disturbed by the collapse of the main device she had used to hold her present relationship, and life in general, at arm's length—namely, the idealized memory of that lover.[56] Her reaction deepens and unfolds after she returns to their cottage, which suggests the real trauma here is not simply her finding him live and lunatic, but the consequent loss of what has been one of her safest sanctums.

Her response as the collapse of her image of the past radiates in her psyche is especially revealing: she isolates herself in the room, locks the door against her husband, and attempts to exclude him utterly by denying her love for him, even denying his right to know what has so upset her. With the collapse of the facade of her memories, she no longer has any excuse to withhold herself from her marriage. The result is an attempt to withdraw from her husband physically and psychologically, epitomized by her telling herself, "She had never loved him. She did not love him now" (*PO*, 130). But at this very moment we are told something that reveals a deeper stratum of her psyche, and that paradoxically may promise some hope for the future:

> But suddenly she lifted her head again swiftly, like a thing that tries to get free. She wanted to be free of it. It was not him so much, but it, something she had put on herself, that bound her so horribly. And having put the bond on herself, it was hardest to take it off. But now she hated everything and felt destructive. (*PO*, 130)

Given Lawrence's mode of presentation of his characters' psyches, it is unlikely the woman explicitly recognizes she is struggling against a self-imposed bond, but this passage does suggest a deeper, self-generated problem than her simply being too enamoured of her memories. And the word "now" implies the destructive hatred she presently feels may be only a phase.

The possibility that the woman is struggling with a self-imposed constraint she wishes to be freed of raises the question of why she has come back to this town and this garden, thus making risky trial of her dreams. On the one hand, her visit to the garden might signal her need of reinforcement by means of the physical presence of the rose garden if she is to continue to hold her marriage relationship at bay. But more positively, her willingness to risk a return to this sanctum may signal some readiness, perhaps unconscious, on her part to make a significant change, a new departure. In any event, the garden she had presumed would serve as a retreat is utterly destroyed for her by the appearance of her ghost lover.

Paradoxically, the young man for whom she now feels hatred is the source of her release from these self-imposed bonds. To say this is not to attribute to Frank any magical power, or any profound understanding of their situation, or even any unusual qualities as a person. It simply recognizes he is the other—an other she herself has chosen—who by virtue of his otherness can do things for her she cannot do for herself. The reason she feels so strongly against Frank at this juncture is her sensing that this "rather small young man" may be crucial to her finding a way to fuller life, and she fears and resents this deeply.[57]

Unlikely as this may at first seem, Frank's response to his wife's crisis may hold out some hope for the future, especially if we compare Frank with several of the less empathetic, more aggressive, and "masculine" characters of some of Lawrence's other stories. (Consider, for example, how Henry Grenfel of "The Fox" would have pursued this woman, had he sensed the terrible vulnerability she now feels.) Though he is deeply hurt and frustrated when she locks the door of their room and denies him any "right" to know why she is so disturbed, Frank does not react viciously or peremptorily to these actions or to her account of her relationship with the vicar's son, part of which is done "to anger him" (*PO*, 131). For one thing, in their confrontation with one another, they have already "made contact" in ways that have shattered their earlier defenses. Running beneath their antagonistic exchanges with one another is a suggestion that their acts are done partly out of an effort to make contact with one another.

When she begins her account of her earlier experiences, we are told, "she began, in a hard voice, as if wilfully to wound him" (*PO*, 130). Subsequently we are told of one of the husband's comments that he said it "brutally, wanting to hurt her into contact with himself" (*PO*, 131). According to the closing paragraph of the story,

> He stood and looked at her. At last he had learned the width of the breach between them. She still squatted on the bed. He could not go near her. It would be violation to each of them to be brought into contact with the other. The thing must work itself out. They were both shocked so much, they were impersonal, and no longer hated each other. After some minutes he left her and went out. (*PO*, 132)

Before we presume this passage signals the end of their marriage, we must "contextualize" it. We should always be wary of statements about Lawrence's characters such as "At last he had learned . . . ," especially when these occur at the ends of chapters or of stories. Such passages almost always represent the character's perspective *in the circumstances, at that particular time*. While the ending of the story presents no obvious resolution, it contains some bases for hope. The breach between them is probably not so wide as it now seems to Frank, and though we cannot confidently predict smooth sailing for this relationship, there is something positive in the recognition of the degree of shock both feel, and in Frank's decision to temporarily leave his wife to come to terms with herself.[58] Their terrible confrontation may well have breached the barriers that have so long separated them, and may provide the basis for deeper and more honest engagement.

"England, My England"

"England, My England" has attracted a considerable amount of critical attention, but much of it has been brief or cursory. This is unfortunate because brief treatment of so complex a story inevitably invites simplification and distortion. Many critics have taken it for granted the story directly reflects an actual biographical situation—that of the family of Madeline Meynell Lucas—and therefore merits little critical attention.[59] Some critics have misread the story's point of view by assuming the sardonic tone and explicit judgments of characters directly reflect Lawrence's own evaluation.[60] Others have presumed the story is Lawrence's depiction of the class struggle in England, and that Egbert's actions are therefore best understood in terms of his class, rather than in terms of the complexity of his person and his situation.[61]

There is more to the story than this, as we shall see if we approach it in its own terms rather than through some preset assumption. Basically the story is about the inevitable tension, even rivalry, between two qualitatively different life modes, two different responses to the questions: What does life require of us? Is life a gift to be enjoyed or a challenge to be met? Is the norm of human experience joy or duty? These two modes (which I shall call the aesthetic and the pragmatic) are represented on the one hand in the attitude of the young Egbert that life is an end in itself, a gift to be enjoyed, and on the other hand the attitude of the Marshalls (especially old Godfrey) that life is a means to some end, a challenge to be confronted, and that we must somehow justify our existence.[62] Lawrence suggests here and elsewhere in his writings that these two modes will never be compatible but that both are necessary to the fullness of life and should exist in balanced polarity. In this story, as the title suggests, Lawrence presents these modes not simply as generic human tendencies, but as aspects of the British character, both necessary to the wholeness of English culture, even though England itself seems to have lost sight of this truth and devotes itself to the pragmatic.

In "England, My England" the balance between the two modes is lost, and the aesthetic mode, embodied in Egbert, collapses. But this imbalance is not presented as the result of a simple power struggle. Egbert's mode loses out not because of an inherent lack of virtue or power, but rather because it comes to accept the pragmatist's (its necessary opponent's) estimate of its own lack of worth, and thus undermined loses faith in itself. The result is Egbert's decline from joy and insouciance to irresponsibility, self-denigration, and finally despair and self-destruction.

The heart of the story, then (though this is not immediately obvious), is Egbert's carefully chronicled decline. To understand this decline, we must realize the story begins in medias res and that more than one-third of it consists of a flashback to the earlier years of the marriage.[63] By the time of the events depicted in the opening paragraphs (that is, seven years into the marriage), important changes have occurred in the relationship between Egbert and Winifred and within Egbert himself, changes rooted in their temperamental differences and promoted by their milieu. As the story opens Egbert has become worried and has "a pleat between his brows"; we are told, "His heart was hard with disillusion: a continual gnawing and resistance. But he worked on. What was there to do but submit!" (*EME*, 5).

These dark feelings are utterly alien to the earlier Egbert—the Egbert who brought to the Grange and to his marriage with Winifred a wonderful blossoming and a careless capacity to delight in life for its own sake. Nor does this earlier insouciance in Egbert imply that he is a wastrel; on the contrary, in the earliest stages of the marriage he contributes something essential if intangible to life at the Grange. To the holly and hawthorn of the Marshall stock, Egbert brings the self-justifying beauty of the rose. To their concern with duty, he brings pleasure and joy. And in these early stages of the marriage he apparently lives his life without feelings of defensiveness or inadequacy. Even old Godfrey's paternalism and his wish to supplement Egbert's insufficient personal income appears not to bother Egbert; indeed, we are told, "Egbert didn't mind being patronized and paid for" (*EME*, 10)—though we learn later that this is not entirely true.

One reason—perhaps the primary reason—it is difficult for us to see Egbert affirmatively, even at these early stages, is the "point of view" in the story. Though not monovocal, it most often speaks from the perspective of the Marshalls or at least reflects their attitude toward life. This perspective can be felt in the statement, "In town Egbert had plenty of friends, of the same ineffectual sort as himself, tampering with the arts, literature, painting, sculpture, music" (*EME*, 10). Certainly this statement does not represent Egbert's self-evaluation, but the reader may not see that neither does it represent an "authorial" evaluation of him. According to the larger perspective behind the story, neither of the attitudes represented by these characters is to be disdained, and both have a valid claim to being English. We are told of the Marshalls, "the girls and the father were strong-limbed, thick-blooded people, true English, as holly trees and hawthorne are English" (*EME*, 7). But of Egbert the narrator says he had "no conception of Imperial England, and Rule Brittania was just a joke to him. He was a pure-blooded Englishman, perfect in his race, and when he was truly himself he could no more have been aggressive on the score of his Englishness than a rose can be aggressive on the score of its rosiness" (*EME*, 27). And we are told of Egbert and Marshall, "Different as the two men were, they were two real Englishmen, and their instincts were almost the same" (*EME*, 28).

The underlying point of view of the story is, then, elusive, refusing to sanction one mode at the expense of the other, even though we might expect to find Lawrence favoring the "aesthete" over the "pragmatist" in this rivalry. This expectation is plausible both because of Lawrence's own disdain for "Imperial England and Rule Britannia" and because of a key passage of his "Study of Thomas Hardy" in which, using images parallel to those in "England, My England," Lawrence asks whether the plant exists for the fruit or the flower and then answers, "Not the fruit, however, but the flower is the culmination and climax, the degree to be striven for" and "The final aim is the flower" (*Study of Thomas Hardy and Other Essays*, 12). That the fruit/flower contrast is appropriate to the Marshalls/Egbert rivalry is shown by Lawrence's efforts to repeatedly link Egbert with the self-justifying flower, as when we are told of him, "He was like a flower in the garden, trembling in the wind of life, and then gone, leaving nothing to show" (*EME*, 12). But the underlying tone is not so easily established, and the strength of the story derives in part from the fine balance of attitude it maintains toward these two modes: neither is finally disdained, both are seen as necessary to the fullness of life.

It does, however, appear that the evaluative statements in the story most often reflect the Marshalls' perspective and thus denigrate Egbert's mode. Why this should be so is not clear, but it seems most likely that the negative tone through which Egbert is presented reflects Lawrence's sense of our cultural psyche's general attitude toward the life mode Egbert manifests, so that this tone replicates the milieu in which any such rivalry must now be carried on. Modern Western culture is founded on and prides itself upon its achievement, its productivity, its control over the forces of nature. As respect for these qualities has grown, our respect for the arts and our ability to treat life as an end in itself have declined. Most modern Westerners are like the Marshalls in their skepticism about the tangibility of the value of the "aesthetic" mode, in their belief that the plant really exists for the fruit rather than for the flower. It seems likely, then, that the generally negative tone taken toward Egbert reflects this bias of our culture.

But the apparent predilection against Egbert seems to exist not simply in the tone but in the very events of the story: how can we respect Egbert or what he represents in the face of his abdication of responsibility in Joyce's accident and his self-destructive, almost groveling acceptance of his father-in-law's advice to join the army? These are perplexing questions, but an answer can be found in the subtle "contextuality" of the story. To understand these puzzling and disturbing actions on Egbert's part, we must empathize as fully as possible with his situation, and we must examine the gradual changes the marriage and Egbert's personality undergo.

In the early months of the marriage Egbert is spontaneous and insouciant, and Winifred values what he brings to their relationship. Egbert is said to have a "delightful spontaneous passion" (*EME*, 7), and we are told that he made the garden "flame with flowers," he "re-created" it (*EME*, 6).[64] And the relation between Egbert and Winifred is described quite positively: "Wonderful then, those days at Crockham Cottage" (*EME*, 8). But while Winifred enjoys this relationship, she feels from the first that the mode of life she experiences with Egbert is somehow lacking, having the temporary, artificial quality of a holiday. Of Egbert's passion for old folk music and old customs, we are told, "Of course in time he would make money in these ways" (*EME*, 7), suggesting that only when it justifies itself financially will his antiquarianism become respectable. In another revealing passage, we learn that "Winifred loved him, loved him, this southerner, as a higher being. A *higher* being, mind you. Not a deeper" (*EME*, 8; emphasis in the original). This higher/deeper distinction is interesting, both for what it reveals about Winifred's underlying attitude toward Egbert and for what it suggests about the subtlety of authorial perspective. The implication is that Winifred views Egbert as somewhat elevated, perhaps ethereal, but ineffectual and lacking in the rootedness and substantiality that defines her father. This categorization and Winifred's implicit assumption that eventually Egbert's pastimes will justify themselves financially show that she has reservations about giving herself wholly to his mode of life. But it is doubtful this judgment rises fully to the surface of her mind, and she might even disavow it if faced directly with it. Further, the ironic tone here suggests an authorial perspective that is amused by Winifred's unwitting condescension, showing that the point of view does not always favor the pragmatic Marshalls.

And for all his insouciance, Egbert is not entirely indifferent to how the Marshalls view him. At first he is self-confident and caught up in the happiness of the marriage. Even his modest income and their partial dependence on old Godfrey seems not to touch him since he believes in, or rather takes for granted, his own pleasure in life and the value of what he brings to Winifred and the cottage. But gradually he becomes aware of Winifred's reservations—her sense that their life together is a wonderful lark but somehow lacking—and this awareness begins subtly to infect Egbert's attitude regarding his own mode of life. Winifred's underlying allegiance, her underlying sense of what is real, is suggested by the narrator's comment, "She loved Egbert with passion. But back of her was the power of her father. It was the power of her father she referred to, whenever she needed to refer" (*EME*, 10).

The gradual surfacing of Winifred's attitude toward Egbert—and his growing awareness of her attitude—is crucial to Egbert's devolution. The Marshalls' denigration of his mode of life affects Egbert's own attitude toward it and causes him to question its value. (The capacity for self-doubt is itself a trait of Egbert's type rather than Godfrey's; were old Marshall to sense someone thought him a fool, he would simply shrug it off, whereas Egbert is more likely to take it to heart, to ponder whether it reveals some defect in him.) One effect of Egbert's self-doubt is his change in attitude toward his increasing financial reliance on old Godfrey so that Egbert "began to get huffy" when it becomes too obvious the Marshalls look down on his incapacity to earn money (*EME*, 10).

The birth of the first child is a turning point in the marriage, precipitating elements that had until then been in solution. The narrator tells us, "After the child was born, it was never quite the same between him and Winifred. The difference was at first hardly perceptible. But it was there" (*EME*, 11). The issue is whether the child is to be reared by Egbert's laissez-faire mode or the more substantial mode of the Marshalls. But the real focus is on Winifred's reaction; the presence of the child brings to the surface her latent misgivings about the quality of their life together, clarifying (for the reader if not for Winifred) the realization that her sense of duty has roots even deeper than her love for her husband (*EME*, 11). Soon Winifred even begins to resent her passion for Egbert (*EME*, 12), as if it were a sign of weakness on her part.

Since Egbert is no more than human, since he does not live hermetically sealed away from his relationships, he cannot help but be affected, and further undermined, by Winifred's withdrawal. He becomes troubled, bitter; he comes to see himself as wicked, perverse, alienated so that "even he himself had to lock up his own vivid life inside himself" (*EME*, 13), and feels he has "seven devils" within himself. Almost inevitably, as his faith in himself erodes, Egbert loses his fine, spontaneous indifference to authority and responsibility, taking on a polarized opposition to whatever qualities he finds embodied in the Marshalls. In contrast, or rather in opposition, to the authority represented by Godfrey and relied upon by his daughters, Egbert becomes "the living negative of power. Even of responsibility.... Egbert would not take the responsibility" (*EME*, 16, 17).

Looking carefully at the context behind the opening scenes of the story enables us to see that the Egbert of the pleated brow and the disillusioned heart has already gone a long way down the road of self-disavowal. And this context too suggests why he responds so poorly, so irresponsibly, to Joyce's accident. Had this accident happened some years earlier, before Egbert began defining himself in opposition to everything represented by the Marshalls, he would likely have responded to it quite differently—not authoritatively, perhaps, but responsibly. But by the time the accident occurs he has set himself against authority and responsibility, so that no matter how much his heart may be anxious about Joyce's knee (*EME*, 21), he will not act; action, authority, and responsibility have been relegated to the Marshalls.

The result, of course, is still further polarization. Winifred becomes more purely the Mater Dolorata, suffering the seven swords in her breast (*EME*, 23); and Egbert becomes more fully the alien, evasive serpent, now turning away even from sympathy (*EME*, 25), an Ishmael (*EME*, p. 26). He has in effect sold himself out entirely and lives now in negation of his own earlier best qualities. It should come as no surprise, then, that when the outbreak of the war provides the opportunity, Egbert carries the process of his self-disavowal to what seems its logical conclusion by enlisting. Here again, his enlistment, amounting virtually to suicide, is something he simply would not have done a few years earlier. But his growing self-estrangement causes him to feel the appropriateness, even the inevitability, of taking actions diametrically opposed to his true nature. We are told that "when the war broke out his whole instinct was against it: against war" (*EME*, 27), and yet he goes directly to old Godfrey and asks whether he should join up, "immediately" following the advice he knows will be given (*EME*, 29). After this, we are told, "An ugly little look came on to his face, of a man who has accepted his own degradation" (*EME*, 29).

It is not clear why Lawrence describes so fully Egbert's military experience, especially his drift toward death.[65] It may be he sensed a similar process at work in our culture or a similar temptation in himself and needed to explore it fully. In any event, the story's closing pages provide a profound and troubling account of what happens in a psyche that has lost faith in itself and turned upon itself. Egbert comes to see himself as doomed, as fated, and feels a self-punishing need to consciously observe the process of his own decline. Yielding himself to the drift toward death, he finds his own dissolution more tangible and more real than any further struggle to maintain his mode of life against overwhelming odds:

> Better the agony of dissolution ahead than the nausea of the effort backwards. Better the terrible work should go forward, the dissolving into the black sea of death, in the extremity of dissolution, than that there should be any reaching back towards life.... Let the black sea of death itself solve the problem of futurity. Let the will of man break and give up. (*EME*, 33)

The story, then, is about a rivalry between two qualitatively different life modes, but the outcome is not the balance or equilibration Lawrence calls for in "The Crown," but the undermining and destruction of one by the other. Not that this unhappy result implies any villainy on the Marshalls' part; they are simply living life in terms of what seems to them most real, most substantial. They can hardly be expected to carry forward the case for Egbert's mode of life any more than one individual in a marriage relationship can be expected to disavow himself or herself in favor of the other: life does not progress that way. And, as the story shows, both of these modes have formed important parts of the English character, and each can still claim to be truly English. But the fact that the equilibrium on which fullness of life depends is displaced in the way that it is, that is, the Marshalls prevail and Egbert not only succumbs but turns against himself, indicates what Lawrence sees as the drift of our culture toward a pragmatism and a pride in triumphing that are healthy when they are one component of a culture, but baneful and life depleting when they become the norm, the sole respected life mode, of the society.

"The Blind Man"

My view of this story rests upon the belief—reached after considerable heuristic trial and error—that the marriage of Maurice and Isabel is a fundamentally sound, even a rich, union.[66] But because of various elements in his personality and in their present situation, Maurice finds himself in need of relationships outside his marriage, and this need draws him into the idea that even Bertie, whom he has never liked, might provide something he lacks. Isabel concurs in the idea of inviting Bertie, but she does so for different reasons than Maurice.

I have already used the opening paragraph of this story to illustrate Lawrence's subtlety in presenting his characters' psychic states. As I said then, the rest of the story simply does not bear out the claim that Bertie is "almost indispensable to [Isabel's] being," and yet this statement does reflect a feeling that exists in Isabel at this time. The feeling may be attributed in part to her immediate situation of active expectation, and to Lawrence's audacious willingness to put into print feelings of his characters that are never sanctioned by articulation and that might even be denied by the character to whom they are attributed. Insofar as this feeling does have roots deeper in her psyche, it expresses a real need for respite Isabel feels, but that need does not arise out of any serious flaw in the marriage.

To understand what lies behind the crisis the story dramatizes and what it is that brings Maurice to his rather unlikely and obviously foredoomed appeal to Bertie, we need to recognize three elements in Maurice's personality and in Maurice and Isabel's marriage situation. There are temperamental differences between Maurice and Isabel— differences that have for the most part enriched their marriage but have recently become the source of problems. First, Maurice has always been more in need of friendships beyond their marriage than has Isabel. Second, Maurice is disposed to turn toward others because of his fears about the effects of his wounding and his blindness on his relationship with Isabel. And third, a more immediate (though temporary) source of his need to turn to someone else is Isabel's pregnancy and her consequent drawing away from him into a private rapport with her unborn child.

While Maurice is the central figure, the story does require us to empathize with Isabel's situation. Isabel on the whole is more content than Maurice to let their marriage be all-sufficing, virtually a world unto itself. She has always felt this way to some extent, and now that she is pregnant she could be totally content within the world of the Grange. There is, however, a problem Isabel feels quite distinctly, even though she does not understand its origin or its nature. While for the most part their life together is rich and even joyful, we are told,

> But as time wore on, sometimes the rich glamour would leave them. Sometimes, after months of this intensity, a sense of burden overcame Isabel, a weariness, a terrible *ennui*, in that silent house approached between a colonnade of tall-shafted pines. Then she felt she would go mad, for she could not bear it. And sometimes he had devastating fits of depression, which seemed to lay waste his whole being. (*EME*, 46–47)

This sounds ominous and might seem to contradict my claim that their marriage is sound. The underlying source of this trouble is not that the marriage is defective, however, but that even the best of all possible marriages cannot provide all the human relationships we may need. And in this regard Maurice and Isabel differ both temperamentally and by virtue of their particular present situation. Maurice, though blind, has always been by nature more gregarious than Isabel, has always wanted some kind of friendship or relationship beyond their marriage. Isabel has never really felt this need, and is consequently puzzled as to why they cannot truly be a world entirely to themselves—or put differently, why she cannot provide all Maurice needs.[67] We are told Isabel's "one great article of faith" is "that husband and wife should be so important to one another, that the rest of the world simply did not count" (*EME*, 48). But Maurice has never totally shared this feeling, and consequently from time to time he wants to invite friends to the Grange. While Isabel is willing to accommodate Maurice, she does not herself feel the need for these others, as is indicated by the narrator's remarks, "She professed herself quite happy and ready to receive *Maurice's friends*. She was happy and ready: the happy wife, the ready woman, in possession. Without knowing why, the friends retired abashed and came no more" (*EME*, 48; my emphasis). The reason "Maurice's friends" retire abashed is that they sense they are not needed, not welcome, and that at least one member of the Pervin household—Isabel, "in possession"—regards them as intruders. Not that any of this is said, but they sense it and "without knowing why" come no more. We should not see this as a judgment against Isabel; it is simply that persons vary in the range of relationships they need, as they do in every other quality.[68]

Similarly, when the rich intensity of their relationship periodically becomes a dark burden—that is, when Isabel senses some need in Maurice she is not fulfilling—her reaction is first to try to supply from herself all Maurice requires, since she does not understand why they cannot be everything to one another. When this effort fails and Isabel seeks some way out, we are told, "She invited friends, she tried to give *him* some further connection with the outer world" (*EME*, 47; my emphasis), but this effort too fails in part for the reason I have already discussed, and in part because their marriage relationship is so deep and rich that other relationships seem trivial by comparison.

What leads to the particular crisis the story turns upon are the other two factors noted above: Maurice's fears about the effects of his blindness, and Isabel's wish to luxuriate in her pregnancy. While Maurice's blindness has in some respects enriched their marriage (I believe what Isabel says to Bertie on pages 58–59), his blindness and his disfiguring scar is the proximate, apparent source of the dark intensity both he and Isabel occasionally feel. Though he has great faith in their relationship, Maurice nonetheless permits his blindness, and the ugly scar associated with it, to infect his confidence in her total acceptance of him.

In another of those passages that sounds authorial but actually reflects a character's (mis)perceptions, Lawrence tells us of Maurice's reaction to his situation. Appropriately, what leads into this passage is his overhearing the voices of Isabel and Bertie below, and feeling "shut out—like a child that is left out" (*EME*, 55). Then we are told:

> He was fretful and beside himself like a child, he had almost a childish nostalgia to be included in the life circle. And at the same time he was a man, dark and powerful and infuriated by his own weakness. By some fatal flaw, he could not be by himself, he had to depend on the support of another. And this very dependence enraged him. He hated Bertie Reid, and at the same time he knew the

hatred was nonsense, he knew it was the outcome of his own weakness. (*EME*, 55)

This passage involves some revelations, and some misperceptions.
First, though purportedly directed at Bertie, it gives us an insight into
how Maurice sometimes feels about his dependence upon Isabel, especially when she tries to hold his dark intensity at some distance, and
more especially now that she is pregnant and dwelling more and more
upon the child she is carrying. The exclusion and even hatred Maurice now directs at Bertie, he occasionally feels toward Isabel, upon
whom he depends on and whom he needs far more than he needs
Bertie. Maurice's perfectly natural misperceptions emerge in his identifying the source of his childish dependence with his blindness, and
his regarding his dependence as a sign of failure. The crucial sentence
is "By some fatal flaw, he could not be by himself, he had to depend
upon the support of another." This dependence Maurice regards as a
weakness, doubtless growing out of his blindness, but Lawrence
wishes us to understand that such need of another person is not in fact
a fatal flaw, but a feature of our inherently social nature. As Lawrence
explains in his essay "We Need One Another," though we often resent it and do what we can to deny or evade it, we cannot be ourselves
without our relationships with others: "We all want to be absolute,
and sufficient unto ourselves. And it is a great blow to our self-esteem
that we simply *need* another human being" (*Phoenix*, 188).

The invitation to Bertie arises from quite different motives in Maurice and Isabel. In Maurice it reflects the virtual desperation of his
need for contact with some other, beyond Isabel. Maurice knows
Bertie well enough from the past to know how utterly different they
are, and should know how unlikely finding real friendship with Bertie
will be, but he nonetheless grasps at this straw. It is not clear what it
is that enables Maurice to believe, or at least to tell himself, that there
is the prospect of a relationship between them. But for the reader it is
obvious even before the terrible scene at the pulping machine that
Bertie is incapable of relating to Maurice.

Isabel is willing to invite Bertie to the Grange partly out of hope
that a relationship between the two men may develop—though she
seems dubious about this possibility from the first. But whether they
become close or not, Bertie will, Isabel hopes, serve to deflect some of
Maurice's terrible intensity away from herself, and this will be a welcome relief. Furthermore, Isabel is willing to invite Bertie because he

will provide her with just the kind of undemanding, null relationship she needs in her present state. Especially given her pregnancy, she has had more than enough of Maurice's intensity, and would find it a relief to have someone around whose presence demands little or nothing from her.

I spoke earlier of Lawrence's characters sometimes indulging in rationalizations, to hide from themselves what their real feelings are. One such instance occurs with Isabel, in regard to Bertie, when we are told, "She loved him—though not in the marrying sense. There was a sort of kinship between them, an affinity. They understood one another instinctively. But Isabel would never have thought of marrying Bertie. It would have seemed like marrying in her own family" (*EME*, 47–48). The fact of the matter is that Isabel has no interest in and very little respect for Bertie as a man, and would never consider marrying him under any circumstances, but she conceals this from herself by the ploy of regarding him as a kinsman, a brother.

The climactic scene between Maurice and Bertie at the pulping machine reveals the depth of Maurice's need and has disturbing implications. The speed with which Maurice turns to Bertie reflects the desperation he feels. Almost immediately he acknowledges to Bertie his misgivings about Isabel's happiness, and asks him about the scar— topics he apparently feels he cannot broach with Isabel, though we know, and Maurice should know, how little these things mean to her. His acknowledgment to Bertie of his fear that he is horrible because of the scar is another instance of Maurice's misconstruing as a function of his particular flaws, a trait all humans share. A sense of unworthiness in the face of love is a generic human trait and does not require a disfigurement to prompt and promote it.

But more disturbing even than the speed of his turning to Bertie is his failure to sense how aghast the lawyer is at his proffered bonding. Maurice has no sense, so deep is his need and so complete his involvement, that he is himself providing virtually all of whatever relationship there might be—suggested by his remark to Bertie, "I thought you were taller" (*EME*, 62)—and that his intense feeling is not in the least reciprocated. Even when the two men return to the house and it is obvious to Isabel that something is very wrong, Maurice has no awareness of Bertie's revulsion. And the implications of Maurice's isolate ecstasy only become more disturbing if we speculate on what is likely to follow. It is hard to imagine Bertie can maintain the facade of any real friendship even sufficiently to mislead a blind man, and the effects on Maurice of realizing the truth about his nonrelationship with Bertie may be devastating.

Unless Bertie and Isabel handle the situation very deftly and Bertie quickly finds some excuse to leave, Maurice will soon realize what a fool he has made of himself—for that is certainly how he will construe it—and the terrible backwash of emotions may well erode his willingness ever again to venture so much with anyone.

"Wintry Peacock"

This story is one of Lawrence's few uses of first-person point of view—especially uncharacteristic during this phase of his career when he had developed his style into so subtle a vehicle of his characters' subliminal, subconscious feelings and needs.[69] I have already argued that third-person indirect presentation is better suited to Lawrence's purposes because first-person narration confines itself to what the narrator can coherently recount, whereas Lawrence is more interested in what lies beneath that level. For most modern writers, first-person point of view becomes a challenge to reveal more than the narrator realizes, making the story an unwitting self-portrait.

For every first-person narrative since James and Conrad, a large part of the challenge for the writer, and of corresponding interest for the reader, is to present the narration so that it is colored by aspects of the narrator's personality of which he is unaware. This is the case with such classic first-person narratives as Conrad's "Heart of Darkness," Sherwood Anderson's "I Want to Know Why," Hemingway's "My Old Man," and Fitzgerald's *The Great Gatsby*. While Lawrence was capable of playing that game, he seems to have regarded such a use of first-person point of view more as a technical tour de force than as an opportunity to carry out meaningful explorations of the characters' struggles with their own subconscious needs—which is his more characteristic subject. "Wintry Peacock" is, however, a Lawrencean first-person narrative in which the narrator is sufficiently characterized that it does behoove us to consider the extent to which this story is "about" the situation and the psyche of the narrator.[70]

Before turning to an analysis of the story, I must glance at certain differences between the version printed in *EME* and the manuscript version, some of them mechanical, but one of relevance to my interpretation. Bruce Steele prints the rejected manuscript portions in his Cambridge edition of *EME*, thus enabling us to make comparisons. First, we can see that not all Lawrence's changes and deletions were made carefully or smoothly; several inconsistencies persist in the printed version that should have been modified when the cuts were made. For example, the slightly puzzling, unprepared-for phrase "she had on the cotton bonnet" (*EME*, 77) refers to a bonnet previously mentioned in the manuscript (see the Cambridge edition of *EME*, 241), but not in the printed version. Similarly, Lawrence originally conceived Elise as French, but later made her Belgian, but in doing so forgot to adjust the reference to her letter "addressed from France" (*EME*, 78).

For my interpretation of the story, the most interesting difference between original manuscript and printed version regards the marital situation of the narrator. The manuscript makes one brief reference to the narrator's wife—he responds to the young woman's question about where he is staying by saying, "Living over at Scargill for the present—my wife and I" (*EME*, 241)—but the story as printed gives no indication the narrator is married. There are several references to "we" or "us" at the house where the narrator is staying, but the identity of the other is not specified: it could be the owner of the house where he is staying. If it were his wife, it seems unlikely there would be no conversation between them, nor even any reference to her for the whole of that long, despondent, snowed-in Thursday. The pronouns from *EME* 83.26 through 84.33 are consistently singular; only when he returns to the house with the bedraggled peacock does the narrator begin to talk in plural terms (*EME*, 84.34).

In any event, the published story gives no hint that the narrator is married or has any substantial relationships with anyone. This is important because the unwitting self-portrait that emerges from this narration is of someone much more an observer of than a participant in relationships, someone unhappy with the quality of his own life, and distinctly ill at ease in relationships with women—a portrait that comports better with a loner than with a married man. While on one level the story is about the marriage relationship of the Goytes, on another level that invites our interest more as we reread the story, it is about the psychology of this viewpoint character, especially about his unease with relationships, and his wish to vicariously observe—though always at a safe distance—the relationship between these cunning, experienced married partners.

From this vantage point, then, the Goyte's marital relationship is not the real focus of the story, though it does of course evoke our interest and require our attention. Alfred has been away for some time, and he has been unfaithful to Maggie. She wishes both to learn specific facts about Alfred's actions from the letter, and to find something that will provide her with ammunition in the skirmishes that will ensue upon his return. While Maggie does not to our knowledge have a lover, she does have her peacocks—especially Joey—and she uses them in ways that obviously elicit anger and jealousy from Alfred. The tenor of the marriage, to judge from the appeals and requests both make of our narrator, is not tranquil, yet there is no reason to deem the marriage a failure. We get the sense that this couple, separated for much of the six years of their marriage, is still sparring, has not yet found—if they ever will—a tranquil modus vivendi. But certainly neither of them has simply succumbed to the other—Maggie's resourcefulness and guile are obvious, and hints indicate their relationship is still a lively contest and that each still appreciates the insouciance and feistiness of the other (see Alfred's "Good for her!" which the narrator regards as "cryptic" [*EME*, 89], and his "She's a little devil, she is. But I shall have it out with her" [*EME*, 90]).

To return to the first-person narrator, several aspects of his personality are worthy of interest. The first involves his distinct unease around Maggie, and his attribution to her of witchlike qualities; the second is his despondency; the third involves his wish to observe at close range and to participate vicariously but not responsibly in the relationship between the Goytes; the fourth is his manipulation of and his final "bonding" with Alfred.

The narrator is both tantalized and intimidated by Maggie. His first notice of her involves a reference to her "preposterously short skirt" (*EME*, 77), and almost immediately afterward he refers to her looking at him "caressively" and in a way that "makes a man lord of the earth" (*EME*, 77). Soon after we have the first of his several references to Maggie as "witch-like" (*EME*, 78; also 80, 83, 84, 85, 87)—something that reveals far more about the narrator's unease in regard to women than it does about Maggie's occult powers. Maggie is not of course above using her female charms to achieve her ends, but she does so in ways that seem naive and transparent rather than subtle and devious; the narrator himself recognizes he "was being cajoled" (*EME*, 78). The narrator's most dramatic statement in regard to Maggie's effect on him in this initial meeting occurs when she hands him the letter:

"She looked too far into me, my wits were gone" (*EME*, 78). The narrator finds himself disoriented by the transparent wiles of the young woman, suggesting an utter naïveté and inexperience on his part.

Another aspect of the narrator's psyche comes to the surface "the morning after this episode," when he awakes to find the valley covered in snow. His response to the scene is appallingly negative and betrays some eddies beneath the current within his psyche. The snow-covered valley another might see as beautiful he describes as "ghastly," and he says, "I felt I was in a valley of the dead. And I sensed I was a prisoner" (*EME*, 83). His morbid attitude is further revealed in his regarding the black and white valley below him as "utterly motionless and beyond life, a hollow sarcophagus" (*EME*, 83). That this strange response is related to "the episode" the day before is indicated by his saying, "I thought of Tible in the snow, of the black, witch-like Mrs. Goyte. And the snow seemed to lay one bare to influences I wanted to escape" (*EME*, 84).

The implication is that the episode with Maggie has stirred a discontent in his soul, suggesting to him the vacuous, deathlike quality of his own world and his own lack of comparable involvement. Yet it has not moved him deeply enough to propel him into closer involvement with Mrs. Goyte. It expresses, that is, the narrator's Prufrock-like sense of the vacuity of his life, but a wish to nonetheless remain aloof. Though deeply despondent, he is not willing to be drawn into what he regards as the disconcerting sphere of Maggie's influence.

Unwilling to involve himself in relationships in any way, he nonetheless wants to feel again the exciting effects of Maggie, and to observe at close range the dynamics of her marriage. Taking the rescued peacock back to Tible, he immediately finds what he is looking for, for he says of Maggie, "She was flushed and handsome, her eyes bright, her hair slack, thick, but more witch-like than ever" (*EME*, 85). Learning Alfred has returned and is responsible for having driven the peacock from the place, the narrator accepts their invitation to come in, enabling him to observe the couple's situation at firsthand. In spite of discovering a relationship between Maggie and her father-in-law that is warm and affectionate, the narrator persists in regarding her as sinister and witchlike (*EME*, 87). As the narrator prepares to leave, Maggie becomes overtly flirtatious with him: "'Must you go?' she asked, rising and coming near to me, standing in front of me, twisting her head sideways and looking up at me. 'Can't you stop a bit longer?—We can all be cosy today, there's nothing to do outdoors.'" ...

Maggie still stood close in front of me, so that I was acutely aware of my waistcoat buttons" (*EME*, 88). Though he knows Maggie means none of what this suggests and is aware that "the moment I went out of her presence I ceased utterly to exist for her—as utterly as I ceased to exist for Joey," he nonetheless feels great unease, saying, "Yet she seemed almost in physical contact with me while I was with her" (*EME*, 88).

In the ensuing scene with Alfred the narrator is much more in his own milieu, much more secure and in control. Furthermore, he subjects Alfred to some of the same manipulation he suffered from Maggie. Fully aware of how badly Alfred needs to know what only he can tell him, the narrator keeps him dangling for some time, observing the other's vulnerability and unease:

> He did not know exactly how to feel. . . . He seemed to be meditating as to what line of action he should take. He wanted to know the contents of the letter: he must know: and therefore he must ask me, for evidently his wife had taunted him. At the same time, no doubt, he would like to wreak untold vengeance on my unfortunate person. . . . And yet I only looked at him, and considered. (*EME*, 89)

Gradually, the narrator reveals to Alfred both the contents of the letter and what his wife has been given to understand, but he does so slowly, savoring his control and Alfred's discomfort at every stage in the process. Given how dramatically he overreads Maggie's slightest motions, he very likely exaggerates as well Alfred's wish to "wreak untold vengeance" on him, or his "subtle malice." Such ideas enable the narrator to feel he has veered dangerously close to a whole array of strong emotions that are fascinating to him. One point he obviously does not fully appreciate is Alfred's response when he is told Maggie "took in" the story she was told, "As much as she took anything else." When Albert laughs and says "Good for *her*," the narrator regards the comment as "cryptic," whereas it expresses Alfred's pleasure that the woman he has married is not totally a fool and has some mind of her own. Of course, he does want to win out over her, but he also wants the contest to be interesting. The narrator has no appreciation or understanding of such psychological symbiosis.

The grinning and then open laughter that emerge as the story ends grows out of a bonding between the two men, as the narrator reveals more clearly what Alfred wishes to know. The narrator first grins to himself, then grins openly, after which Alfred responds with a grin and then a laugh; the story ends with both in open laughter. But though these two men are briefly linked by this laughter and by their having conspired against the female, their parting returns them to entirely different situations. Alfred, whose "loud burst of laughter... made the still, snow-deserted valley clap again," is going back to a contest with a worthy opponent, going back to an array of emotions, some of which he doubtless finds less than pleasing (his wife's flaunting of her relationship with the peacock),[71] but real emotions nonetheless. The narrator is going back to his own desolation and to his depressed imaginings of witchlike women and men who are capable of holding their own against them.[72]

"You Touched Me"

"You Touched Me" is another story about the surfacing of subterranean needs in characters, involving both Hadrian and Matilda in emotions they cannot understand or articulate.[73] In this respect it is similar to many other Lawrence works; critics have specifically noted parallels with character relationships and themes in "The Fox."[74] But I regard those parallels differently from most critics, seeing in both these stories Lawrence's exploration of certain limitations and costs associated with traditional ideas of masculinity. Both these stories involve a returned soldier and depict a male character whose emotions run deeper than he can understand, and in both the male character tries to construe his needs and motives in conventionally masculine terms. But especially in Hadrian's response to Matilda, there are feelings—new sensations in his psyche growing out of the tenderness he has felt in her touch of his brow—that cannot be accommodated to traditional masculinity.

Before delving deeper into Hadrian's feelings, I will consider Matilda's situation. It requires no great subtlety to see that Matilda has life needs not satisfied by the moribund situation at the pottery house. The closing of the pottery deprives her of a sustaining activity. While the two sisters claim to like the new, quieter situation of the closed pottery much better, Lawrence is explicit about the ambivalence beneath the surface of their feelings. He tells us, "But whether the two Rockley girls really liked it better, or whether they only imagined they did, is a question" (*EME*, 92), and notes, "They did not quite realize how they missed" the activity and noise of the once-bustling pottery. He further suggests this quietness has had its effects on the psyches of these two women when he tells us, "This quiet household, with one servant-maid, lived on year after year in the Pottery House.... Outside in the street there was a continual racket of the colliers and their dogs and children. But inside the pottery wall was a deserted quiet" (*EME*, 93). Lawrence also tells us something important about the women's life situation by declaring, "Matilda and Emily were already old maids" (*EME*, 92).[75]

Lawrence is also clear about the disquieting effect on the women of Hadrian's return after his service in the war. While they try to regard Hadrian as nothing more than the Charity Home boy their father brought into the house when he was six years old, and thus a thoroughly known quantity and their clear inferior, they are "fluttered" by him and even "a little afraid" of him (*EME*, 94). Revealing too is their preparation for his arrival, and their mortification when he appears earlier than expected to find them in their cleaning garb. Matilda especially gives thought to how she will receive Hadrian and impress him, and dresses herself scrupulously, including rouge and jewelry (*EME*, 96–97). And Lawrence says explicitly that Hadrian's "man's voice so deep and unexpected was like a blow to Cousin Emily" (*EME*, 95). In their talk between themselves about Hadrian, Matilda and Emily are contemptuous and "sarcastic," but they are clearly fascinated with him.

Why Matilda rather than Emily emerges as the active figure in the story is not entirely clear. In contrast to the situation in "The Fox," where there is an obvious difference between the two women—Banford wishes to continue the status quo but March is obviously restive—in this story both Emily and Matilda are dissatisfied with their life situation and both are agitated by Hadrian's prospective return. Nor does Hadrian at first seem more strongly attracted to Matilda than to Emily. From what we know of them, it might as well have been Emily as Matilda who commits the crucial act of touching Hadrian. Later in the story Emily does express suspicion and animosity toward Hadrian, but Matilda might also have had such feelings had a relationship emerged between Hadrian and Emily. Emily does say, though, "You go up and get dressed, our Matilda. I don't care about him. I can see to things, and you can talk to him. I shan't" (*EME*, 96), and the earlier comparison/contrast with the biblical Mary and Martha (*EME*, 93) suggests Emily sees herself as more devoted than Matilda to quotidian tasks.

In any event, that Matilda is the one who commits the touch is prima facie evidence she feels the needs the act expresses more strongly than Emily. Moreover, that the act of touch is not sheer accident is suggested by several details of the story. Her father's move from his bedroom to the morning room downstairs (*EME*, 95) could not have taken place without Matilda's knowledge, or presumably her assistance. And the visit to her father's bedroom comes not on the first night of Hadrian's visit, but on the second (*EME*, 98), after Matilda has spent some time with her father, presumably in his new quarters (*EME*, 98).

Of Hadrian's feelings toward these sisters prior to the event of the touch, we are told little, and there is virtually nothing to suggest he has anything other than an independent and self-interested attitude toward the household. But after the touch we are told a good bit about his attitude regarding both that event and Matilda—more than Hadrian is capable of realizing. In his reaction to this disturbing event, we have another instance of a Lawrencean character trying to accommodate disturbing new feelings by telling himself things congruent with his previous life attitudes and image of himself. Lawrence invites us to explore the depths of Hadrian's reaction by telling us, "He had a keen memory stinging his mind [of the touch], a new set of sensations working in his consciousness. Something new was alert in him" (*EME*, 100). Lawrence provides a clue to what this new element is when he says "the soft, straying tenderness of her hand on his face startled something out of his soul. He was a charity boy, aloof and more or less at bay. The fragile exquisiteness of her caress startled him most, revealed unknown things to him" (*EME*, 100). This phrasing suggests this story, like *Lady Chatterley's Lover*, has to do with learning to have the courage to be tender.

These unknown things touch this young man in a way utterly new to him, thus hinting at elements unexpected in someone so independent and aggressive. But when Hadrian reflects on what this experience means, he approaches it in terms more consistent with his image of himself as a charity boy and a soldier, that is, in orthodox masculine terms of control, possession, and mastery. He even tries to understand the new qualities he has sensed in Matilda by denying their femininity and seeing them as qualities in the old man Rockley as well. The following paragraph reflects the various levels of Hadrian's psychology and the devices he uses to accommodate the disturbingly novel elements in his experience to more familiar, conventionally masculine modes of response:

> He looked at her curiously. She was not beautiful, her nose was too large, her chin was too small, her neck was too thin. But her skin was clear and fine, she had a high-bred sensitiveness. This queer, brave, high-bred quality that she shared with her father. The charity boy could see it in her tapering fingers, which were white and ringed. The same glamour that he saw in the elderly man he saw now in the woman. And he wanted to possess himself of it, he wanted to make himself master of it. As he went about through the old pottery-yard, his secretive mind schemed and worked. To be master of that strange soft delicacy such as he had felt in her hand upon his face—that was what he set himself toward. He was secretly plotting. (*EME*, 100)

Hadrian construes the situation as a challenge, a battle of wills. What he does not realize and would probably deny is that his own deeper psyche is "secretly plotting" in ways his conscious, conventional mind is not aware of, because that deeper psyche wants to maintain contact with Matilda's tenderness and sensitivity. Hadrian's conventional mind invokes class distinctions and a battle of wills through which he can "master" the Rockleys and "possess" both the pottery yard and those distinctive life qualities he associates with them. Those are the kinds of motives his competitive, masculine self can understand and sanction, and so these are the motives he tells himself he is secretly plotting in terms of.

The "social climbing" aspect of Hadrian's motives is especially interesting because it proves to be so superficial. Twice Hadrian thinks of the "high bred" quality he associates with Matilda and her father, and being the charity boy he is, this quality presumably has tangible appeal for him. But the subsequent account shows what most fascinates and attracts Hadrian is not wealth or even social status, but the new dimension of tenderness he has felt through Matilda's touch. Thus a story that seems on the surface to give such importance to issues of social class turns out to be about deeper and more perennial human needs.

The inadequacy of this self-deluding account of Hadrian's motives is suggested by a later paragraph that reflects the confused processes within Hadrian's psyche. In spite of his having "secretly plott[ed]" to make himself master of the pottery yard, Hadrian seems truly taken aback by Emily's accusation that he is after her father's money. We are told,

> He turned his back on her, to think. It had not occurred to him that they would think he was after the money. He *did* want the money— badly. He badly wanted to be an employer himself, not one of the employed. But he knew, in his subtle, calculating way, that it was not for money he wanted Matilda. He wanted both the money and Matilda. But he told himself the two desires were separate, not one. He could not do with Matilda, *without* the money. But he did not want her *for* the money. (*EME*, 104)

Hadrian himself is not clear about what he really wants, but it is not simply the money.

Interestingly, Matilda too is shocked by Emily's explicit claim that Hadrian wants the money: "The thought that Hadrian merely wanted the money was another blow to Matilda. She did not love the impossible youth—but she had not yet learned to think of him as a thing of evil. He now became hideous to her mind" (*EME*, 103). This suspicion becomes an impediment—though, as we shall see, not the most serious one—their relationship must circumvent.

Both Matilda and Hadrian find in one another something worth valuing and worth cultivating, but neither of them is clear about what that something is, partly because the needs they are experiencing run so deep in their psyches, partly because each of them tries to comprehend this novel situation by reducing it to familiar terms. Matilda (her needs implicitly pressed upon her by her dull, quiet situation) is drawn by Hadrian's vitality, his independence, his naive self-confidence about his "equality" with others, and his ability to make his way in the world. She senses there is something to him other than defensiveness and self-importance—that there is something *worthy* of tenderness.

The episode of touch on which the story turns, then, is not a pathetic or ludicrous grasping at a straw by two utterly incompatible people; rather, the act and the response occur between two people who know one another quite well—they did after all live together in this house for some nine years before Hadrian's departure—and who sense in one another the possibility of something more than appears on the surface, even to themselves.

Before looking at one other distinctive and troublesome element of this situation, we should assess the assets and liabilities of their potential relationship. Working in their favor is that both Hadrian and Matilda are people of some depth who are dissatisfied with their present life situation and are thus (more or less consciously) looking for a new dimension to their lives. Matilda is almost consciously aware of the lack in her life and of the need expressed by her touching Hadrian; she claims it to have been a mistake—though of course she had known of her father's relocation—but senses nevertheless that it carries meaning for her. Hadrian, before the touch, was much less aware of the lack in his own life, and had to be awakened to it by that strange event—but as he tells Matilda "If you wake a man up, he can't go to sleep again because he is told to" (*EME*, 106).

But if Hadrian more or less "realizes" he has been awakened by the qualities he experienced in the touch, he is still responding to those qualities in terms of the masculine traits that have got him where he is—toughness, self-reliance, plotting—and that will have to be ameliorated if the relationship with Matilda is going to develop. What Matilda has to contend with is, first of all, her own habitual passivity, which might cause her to regard Hadrian as her "savior" from her life of dullness, and, second, the bitterness that has arisen over her father's change of will and Emily's accusation that Hadrian is simply out for the money. Given the depths of each other's psyches they have tapped, the chances of Hadrian and Matilda's overcoming these vestigial attitudes are good.

But the young couple also faces another stumbling block to their relationship—namely, old Mr. Rockley's frustration and anger and its effects. His actions add a complication absent from many of Lawrence's stories about couples trying to forge a new relationship—though there are analogous characters in some other works. Old Rockley is a male version of a character more often presented as a female type, the old woman who would live parasitically on the lives of the next generation.[76] (Perhaps the clearest example in the short stories is Pauline Attenborough in "The Lovely Lady.") Though Lawrence does not fully develop old Rockley's character, we are told early on that he directs a great deal of anger at his household of women (*EME*, 93), and this anger prompted him to adopt Hadrian. But his acts in the story are removed from that adoption by many years and seem to originate in his wish to use Hadrian as a surrogate through whom he can control his remaining daughters, and extend the sphere of his influence beyond the grave. He seems revivified by this prospect, for when Hadrian first proposes marrying Matilda, and Rockley begins to dwell upon it, we are told, "He had flushed, and looked suddenly more alive" (*EME*, 101).

It is of course Hadrian himself who unwisely brings old Rockley into the relationship. Since Hadrian construes the relationship with Matilda so much as a challenge, a battle of wills, he is willing even to invite the assistance of old Rockley in order to win out. He does not see that old Rockley is himself so bitter and vengeful that he will be more of a liability than an asset, finally turning his wish to control even upon Hadrian himself. That the old man's desire for control, for ownership, has by the end of the story extended even to Hadrian, is shown by his saying, "Ay, my lad, I'm glad you're mine" (*EME*, 107). And that the old man is using Hadrian as a surrogate is quite clear from his instructions that Matilda should kiss her father (for the first time in many years), and then his immediate instruction that she kiss Hadrian. So while he has enabled Hadrian to win out over Matilda, he has also introduced fractious forces into their relationship that Hadrian had not bargained for.

The sources of old Rockley's terrible wish to revenge himself on his family of women are not fully clarified; after all, his situation is not what the story is about. He is, though, an additional impediment to the relationship of Matilda and Hadrian, and his influence on their nascent relationship is pernicious. What he puts Hadrian and Matilda (and Emily) through will doubtless complicate their relationship for some time, constituting a real stumbling block to their learning to believe in their mutual need, to trust one another, to have the courage of their tenderness.

"Two Blue Birds"

"Two Blue Birds" is one of my favorites among Lawrence's stories, because of its poignant portrait of Mrs. Gee and the subtle, elusive tone through which it is presented.[77] I know from having read scores of student papers that the authorial perspective and the tone of the story are difficult to pin down, and that grasping the underlying situation among the characters requires a finely adjusted perspective. This is one Lawrence story that calls for trying out various perspectives, various hypothetical readings. Finding the most satisfactory perspective involves speculation and inference about what brought about the present situation, and about what most deeply motivates the characters—including things they themselves do not understand. With so subtle a story, a slight adjustment of perspective can reveal unexpected new dimensions.

The situation within the Gee household is easily misconstrued, and we can be misled as to who is the "villain," who the "heroine"—that is, which of the characters is trying to protect or insulate himself from life's demands, and which one is trying, however imperfectly, to continue to risk living as fully as possible. But once the proper *point d'appui* is discovered, the main lines of the dramatic situation emerge, and we come to understand and sympathize with the desperate situation in which Mrs. Gee finds herself.

Here, as in "England, My England," the tone the narrative voice often assumes is problematic, and the difficulty in discerning the characters' situation arises in part from uncertainty as to whose perspective this jocular, satirical tone represents and at whom its barbs are directed. For the most part, this tone represents the sophisticated attitude the "modernist" milieu takes toward marriage, toward meaningful commitment to another person. Moreover, this flippant tone represents the attitude Mrs. Gee feels she should herself be able to take toward what is happening in her life.

But in spite of Mrs. Gee's defensiveness about her own seriousness, and her sense that she may be making a fool of herself, she cannot regard with insouciance the disconcerting changes in her life in recent years. Once we see through the facade of the attitude she purports to assume and realize the desperateness of her situation, and the seriousness of what is at stake for her, we sympathize with her all the more deeply, and so the final effect of this flippant tone is to render even more poignant the portrait of this inescapably unmodern woman.[78]

The simple-sounding, formulaic phrasing of the story's opening sentences suggests some kinship with the "fabulistic" stories of Lawrence's later period. In some of these stories the fabulistic tenor is pervasive, rendering the story quite different from his intensively psychological earlier work; the most successful such story is "Rocking-Horse Winner," discussed next. In the present case, however, this quality does not pervade the story, which remains as psychologically realistic and subtle as any. Here the fablelike opening (reminiscent of Hawthorne, with whom Lawrence has some affinities of technique) has two functions, neither of which attenuates the dense psychological texture of the story. First, this opening enables Lawrence to deftly establish certain givens of the narrative situation before he homes in on what is really of interest to him here. We are told, that is, that the woman "loved her husband" and that they "felt, in some odd way, eternally married to one another" (*CSS*, 513)—both of which are quite true. Second, the fablelike quality of the opening suggests Lawrence is presenting a story in which the characters play typical parts—and that these modernist "types," have counterparts in many other times and places. "Two Blue Birds" is thus a modernist fable in which the Gees are playing roles—potentially farcical roles, the narrative tone suggests—reflective of some recurrent cultural schema.

In this regard, in his essay "Do Women Change?" Lawrence makes some relevant observations. Making the general point that human experience varies little from age to age, he says, "All that varies is the proportion of 'modern' people to all the other unmodern sorts, the sophisticated to the unsophisticated. And today there is a huge majority of sophisticated people. And they are probably very little different from all other sophisticated people of all the other civilizations, since man was man" (*Phoenix II*, 539). (A few paragraphs later, Lawrence says, "Modernity or modernism isn't something we've just invented. It's something that comes at the end of civilizations" [*Phoenix II*, 540]). The generic, fablelike opening suggests, that is, that these characters are typical of their milieu, and that the story might well be subtitled "A Modern Situation."[79]

The problem with Mrs. Gee, however, is that she really is not a modern woman, though she tries very hard to be one, claiming to take an attitude toward her marital situation far more nonchalant and sophisticated than she actually feels. And in this she exemplifies another problem Lawrence comments on in the essay "Master in His Own House"—what he calls the problem of mass thinking, as against individual thinking. Lawrence illustrates the problem through the dictum "A man must be master in his own house," which he says carries weight for us only so long as we keep it generic and do not think in terms of our particular situation. The mass apothegm Mrs. Gee is wrestling with is something like "No modern woman really *needs* her husband's love and attention," but as the story shows she has failed utterly to live up to this dictum. One point of interest in this story, then, is how the woman's feelings about the crisis in her life are colored and confused (perhaps even partly generated) by her awareness of her modernist situation and by her sense of her marriage as a modern marriage. We come to understand that the forces acting on Mrs. Gee are both personal and cultural. Mrs. Gee, that is, is struggling not just with certain traumatic changes in her personal relationships, but also with perceiving these changes through a received cultural agenda: the agenda of the modern, sophisticated woman.

On the personal level she is torn between real love for and need of her husband, and her inability any longer to make contact with him. On the level of her cultural self she is torn between her old-fashioned wish to acknowledge to herself how much she needs this marriage, and her contrary wish to play the role of the footloose modern woman, unconstrained by fidelity and too sophisticated to be deeply committed to her marriage. She is, then, to some extent a victim of modern modes, modern clichés. We are told of "her strange [by modern standards] yearning to be loyal and faithful" (*CSS*, 513), and are explicitly told that "Her gallant affairs were part of her modern necessity" (*CSS*, 514).

Like "England, My England," "Two Blue Birds" begins in the middle of things, but here we are told much less about the background situation and so must infer more. But if we attend carefully to the implications of what we are told, we can arrive at a working hypothesis. We are told the Gees "had been married for the last dozen years, and couldn't live together for the last three or four" (*CSS*, 514), which means they had been married some eight or nine years before their problems arose. Judging both from Mrs. Gee's personality and from her apparent puzzlement as to what has gone wrong, those first eight or nine years were good ones; that is, she does not seem the type to have languished in a nonrelationship, and it is clear she feels there has been some distinct change. Moreover, we are told explicitly that "Of course she had had good times with him, in the past, before—ah! before a thousand things, all amounting really to nothing" (*CSS*, 519). It was presumably during this eight or nine years that the Gees came to be as fully married as the opening paragraph of the story indicates.

What, then, happened three or four years ago? Since Mrs. Gee is the one wrestling to revivify the relationship, it seems the withdrawal was initiated, however passively, by Mr. Gee. I suggest that, for reasons unknown even to himself, Mr. Gee became intimidated and began to protect and insulate himself from all meaningful life demands and challenges. To what extent his fears and withdrawal stemmed from problems with his writing is not clear, but that his present-day caution and protectiveness do extend to his work is obvious. Gee is a novelist, having published one novel some years ago, and there is good evidence he remains a man of some wit, some cleverness. Nor is he lazy—apparently he does write, or dictate—many hours every day. But instead of working actively on another novel, he is writing an article on "The Future of the Novel" (*CSS*, 523), and the snippet we hear from this dictation is more than enough to confirm Mrs. Gee's judgment that Gee's work has gone into decline: "In every novel there must be one outstanding character with which we always sympathise—with *whom* we always sympathise—even though we recognise it—even when we are most aware of the human frailties" (*CSS*, 521). Add this to the episode in which Mr. Gee has to caution the devoted Miss Wrexall against taking down his offhand remark about the blue tits (*CSS*, 522), and we have confirmation not only of the flaccid nature of the "creative" process, but a hint as well as the pernicious effects of the devotion of the Wrexalls.

But Mr. Gee is no longer the man he was during the first years of the marriage. He has become cautious, tentative, has lost the active energy and engagement in life and in his writing that probably attracted Mrs. Gee in the first place and sustained them during the early years of their marriage.

Mrs. Gee quite correctly senses Cameron is moving toward homeostasis, and thus she understands the effects of the Wrexalls on him to be pernicious. So successful are they in providing for his every need that it becomes virtually impossible for Mrs. Gee to make any impression on him, to regain his attention. And she is quite right too in her instinct that husband and wife owe something more to one another than being able to be relied upon.

In response to her husband's puzzling withdrawal, Mrs. Gee has tried a number of ploys to regain his attention, from spending his money to having affairs. But none of this succeeds either in attracting Mr. Gee or in assuaging her own need for him. What puzzles and irritates Mrs. Gee is (as she puts it) "Why had she such an extraordinary hang-over about him? Just because she was his wife?" (*CSS*, 519). Modern woman that she aspires to be, she cannot understand why she cannot be content with the "modern" marriage into which their union has evolved. Reluctant to admit she still very much loves and needs her husband, she continues to puzzle over why her affairs with other men yield so little and why she still must take her husband so seriously (*CSS*, 519).

Thus the story turns on Mr. Gee's withdrawal from his marriage (and his work), and on Mrs. Gee's response to this withdrawal. Mrs. Gee does not of course understand what is happening to them; all she knows is that the quality of the life they once had is no longer there, and that she finds it increasingly harder to keep up any vital contact with her husband. She also senses, though less clearly, how much she continues to need him and to hope for a renewal of the relationship they once had. When she resorts to various devices to regain her husband's attention—she has affairs, she buys things and has the bill sent to him—Mr. Gee's response is simply to insulate himself ever more securely from any disturbing influences, personal or artistic.

The crisis of the story arises when Mrs. Gee decides her husband's homeostasis, so wonderfully sustained by Miss Wrexall and her family, cannot be permitted to go unchallenged and makes a frontal attack on it. This is not to imply that Mrs. Gee has carefully planned the scene in the garden; the idea of a confrontation springs spontaneously to her mind after seeing the two fighting tits disturb Cameron's equanimity (*CSS*, 522). One thing that makes us sympathize with Mrs. Gee is the naïveté and vulnerability behind the facade of her secure, peremptory manner. In reality she is struggling to understand why her life has changed as it has, and is very frightened and vulnerable. Nor, in the climactic scene, does Mrs. Gee know exactly what she is "accusing" her husband and Miss Wrexall of—whether of a sexual liaison (which seems unlikely), or of writing Mr. Gee's works (which seems unlikely as well, but which succeeds better at getting his attention [*CSS*, 525–26]), or of having ruined him by providing for his every need. Mrs. Gee's aim is simply to rock the boat of this ménage with sufficient vigor so that its occupants must abandon it and swim for their lives, in the hope that Cameron will swim toward her.

It seems unlikely, however, that she achieves her aim, for as is often the case with Lawrence's endings, we are left uncertain what the outcome will be. In my view, Cameron's homeostasis is so firmly in place, his fear of future failure so intimidating, that he will not be jolted into taking upon himself again the demands of the marriage relationship or of the risks of his profession as novelist—aspects of experience that in his mind are doubtless inextricably intertwined. Whether the Wrexall crew will survive Mrs. Gee's accusations is harder to say, but in this modernist milieu there are always those to be found who wish to be a doormat—especially for a famous novelist—and so Miss Wrexall is easily replaceable. Mrs. Gee's future is the real issue, and I believe that after she gains some perspective on this episode, she will realize that if she does not wish to become a pillar of salt, she must turn her back on this relationship that has meant so much to her, and leave without a backward glance this husband whom she loves and strike out into the unknown. Otherwise she will crystallize, and for a woman of such vigor and promise who has just turned 40, that would be a great waste indeed.

One image strand helpful in understanding the wife is that relating to Lot's wife and her crystallization. By the end of the story we see that in spite of her real attachment to Mr. Gee—her love for him—he has become so insulated that he is virtually incapable of a meaningful relationship. Even if the wife has succeeded in fouling up the smooth working of the Wrexall machine, she has not succeeded in jolting Cameron back into life, and so she has no choice, young as she is, but to walk away from the household without looking back. We are told at one point that the wife "stood . . . in an attitude characteristic of her, half-turning back to the little secretary, half averted. She half turned her back on everything" (*CSS*, 523). But if she wishes to save herself from crystallizing totally, she must now no longer look back at her marriage of the last dozen years, but must truly turn her back on it and walk off into whatever she can create for herself in the future.

In retrospect, then, this story does have an almost fablelike simplicity: There was a young couple who were happily married, but the husband grew frightened and withdrew. The wife, puzzled by the change in their lives, wondered whether the fault lay in herself. So she tried desperately to regain their earlier joy, but the husband only became more distant. Then she saw that the husband was truly changed, and she had to go on by herself.

"The Rocking-Horse Winner"

Those who categorize Lawrence's short stories usually classify "The Rocking-Horse Winner" as a fable, or even a supernatural story, and it is true that Lawrence wrote it for a collection entitled *The Ghost Book*.[80] But while Paul's gift for knowing the winners is not susceptible to rational explanation—nor does the story compromise itself by suggesting that it is—the story is not so simply supernatural as "Glad Ghosts," "The Border Line," or "The Last Laugh." Moreover, its supernatural element is wonderfully integrated with its astutely psychological and social dimensions. The story's great genius lies in its seamless interweaving of the "supernatural" with the quite believable problems of the family and with realistically presented dialogue and psychological relationships among the characters.

Attending to the story's skillful integration of these elements reminds us of how continuous a shading off there is in Lawrence's fiction from the realistic stories, to what Janice Harris calls the "visionary stories" (a category involving examples as widely different as "The Prussian Officer," "The Blind Man," and "The Border Line" [*Short Fiction of D.H. Lawrence*, 6–8]), to the "supernatural" stories. Consider, for example, the unlikeliness, the unrealism, of the events central to "The Horse-Dealer's Daughter," or "You Touched Me," or of the killing of Banford in "The Fox," or even of Henry's killing of the fox; Lawrence's works contain innumerable examples of events that strain credulity.[81]

One persistent testimony of all his works is that when dealing with the psyche, especially with its unplumbed depths, it is not easy to draw a line between what is "realistic" and what is not. I point this out not to ameliorate the supernatural element in "The Rocking-Horse Winner," but rather to suggest that, especially given the smooth blending it achieves, the effect of "The Rocking-Horse Winner" is not to make us wonder about ghosts, but to reflect on how strange the workings of the psyche can be.

The opening paragraph does have a "fabulistic" quality, both in its style and in its deft sketching of the basic elements of the situation:

> There was a woman who was beautiful, who started with all the advantages, yet she had no luck. She married for love, and the love turned to dust. She had bonny children, yet she felt they had been thrust upon her, and she could not love them. They looked at her coldly, as if they were finding fault with her. And hurriedly she felt she must cover up some fault in herself. Yet what it was that she must cover up she never knew. Nevertheless, when her children were present, she always felt the centre of her heart go hard. This troubled her, and in her manner she was all the more gentle and anxious for her children, as if she loved them very much. Only she herself knew that at the centre of her heart was a hard little place that could not feel love, no, not for anybody. Everybody said of her: "She is such a good mother. She adores her children." Only she herself, and her children themselves, knew it was not so. They read it in each other's eyes. (*CSS*, 3: 790).

This first paragraph deserves quoting in its entirety because it embodies several of the subtleties and complexities, some of them unappreciated, of Lawrence's "fabulous" mode. Just as in the opening of a fairy tale, the omniscient author tells categorical things about the characters they could not realize about themselves, so here Lawrence apparently tells us about the inmost heart of the mother, how she really feels about her children, in spite of appearances and perhaps even self-deception: "she could not love them." The situation is not so fairy-tale simple, however, for even in this fabulistic paragraph we find one of Lawrence's characteristic complexities of point of view, especially in the sentence, "Only she herself knew that at the centre of her heart was a hard little place that could not feel love, no, not for anybody." For the claim that this sentence makes is not borne out by the story, and we must finally recognize it represents not the authorial truth about the woman, but one of her own deepest fears. That she does in fact love her son Paul is shown in several ways, among them her almost "supernatural" rapport with him while she is at the party. So while certain events of the story are undeniably supernatural and the opening is traditionally fabulistic, readers still find themselves challenged by subtleties of point of view and by the characters' feelings and motives that are characteristic of Lawrence's most purely "psychological" stories.

Moreover, parts of the story are handled in rigorously realistic fashion—for example, the mother's misgivings about her feelings at the party, and her acknowledgment of how contrary to "common sense" her feelings are. Realistic also are the discussions between Basset and Uncle Oscar and Paul about the boy's gift. Uncle Oscar's attitude throughout is a rigorous skepticism, ameliorated only by his discovery that the boy does, inexplicably, have the ability to pick the winners. And this realistic dimension is reinvoked in Uncle Oscar's final observation: "poor devil, poor devil, he's best gone out of a life where he rides his rocking horse to find a winner" (*CSS*, 3:804).[82]

The first paragraph also illustrates the merging of the psychological (or "psychic"?) and the supernatural in its introduction of two words crucial to the meaning of the story: "luck" and "love." In order to appreciate the subtlety of "category-clouding" (between realistic and supernatural) introduced by these terms, we need to ask ourselves what we think about the entities represented by these two simple four-letter words.

Luck is especially problematic for the modernist worldview. How do we really feel about it? Do we "believe" in it—do we think luck is anything real? We do commonly wish others "good luck" (far more often nowadays than we *pray* for them), and we speak of something good happening as a "lucky break." But whether for most of us luck represents anything other than the statistically incalculable is doubtful, and we would probably regard with amusement or disdain anyone—say, an addicted gambler—who believed in luck as something tangible enough to challenge statistical realities.

We might similarly ask how we feel about love—certainly an idea, an ideal, that has been invoked and respected in Western culture for many centuries. But do we really believe in the possibility of a relationship between two discrete people so strong as to reorient the personality and to contravene self-interest, or is such an idea sheer romanticism and "supernaturalism"? Even young people today seem skeptical of the reality, or at least of the power, of love. Nor should this be so surprising when sociobiology has shown us how naive and unlikely such a thing as "altruism" is. Certainly, given the claims traditionally made for it, love seems to us sophisticated, realistic moderns a rather dubious entity. Here in the first two sentences of this fablelike opening paragraph, Lawrence raises, in ways that will become more important as this story unfolds and we sense the strange connection that exists in Paul's psyche between luck and love, questions about what is realistic and what is supernatural.

While the most overtly supernatural aspect of the story is Paul's knowledge of the winners, this is surrounded by other questionable things, of which luck and love are only two. We are told that the house is "haunted by the unspoken phrase: *There must be more money! There must be more money*," and that the "children could hear it all the time, though nobody said it aloud" (*CSS*, 3:791). Are we to regard this voice as a "supernatural" presence? The description suggests that we do, and yet we need not invoke such an explanation. Surely we can believe that in any household the children are subtly responsive to the unspoken needs and tensions of their elders, and in this household the children readily sense their parents' need for more money.[83]

Another questionably realistic event in this story is the mother's feeling about Paul as the crisis approaches—her "strange seizures of uneasiness about him," the "sudden anxiety about him that was almost anguish" (*CSS*, 3:802). This feeling reaches its height two nights before the Derby: she is at a party in town, when, we are told "one of her rushes of anxiety about her boy, her first-born, gripped her heart till she could hardly speak. She fought with the feeling might and main, *for she believed in common sense*. But it was too strong. She had to leave the dance and go downstairs to telephone to the country" (*CSS*, 3:802; my emphasis). The surprised governess assures her that all is well, but in fact it is not, for the process that will result in Paul's death has already begun. In spite of the disavowals of the opening paragraph, the mother is struggling here with her *love* of her son—something "natural" enough, but rendered problematic for her by her deep confusion of values, by her lack of faith in her capacity to love, and by her idea that these feelings violate "common sense."

In this story that plays so subtly with questions of the natural and the supernatural, the most subtle intersection between the two categories takes place in the psyche of young Paul, specifically in regard to his understanding of those crucial terms "love" and "luck." Young Paul is deeply concerned about his mother and wishes to do whatever he can to help her achieve happiness. When he comes to understand from her that the problem in their family is a lack of *luck*, his *love* for her—perhaps a "supernatural" quality, especially given the degree to which Paul feels it—takes on such intensity that it leaps the categories and becomes inordinate *luck*. With this luck, born of his desperate love, he will set right what has gone wrong in his family, the "haunting" all the children have sensed. The result is of course predictable, even before the story spells it out. Paul's inordinate luck, deriving its strength from his desperate love, is not sufficient to still the voices or set the situation in the house right. The parents' confusion of values is so deep and fundamental that it engulfs all the young boy's efforts.

All that Paul can do in response is to try harder, to transform yet more of that profound love he feels for his mother into luck. However, even his amazing store of love—the natural endowment of the child—is not sufficient to sustain an unfailing stream of luck. By trying even harder, he can still sometimes force the luck into being—though by now the demands of that process are sapping his physical as well as his psychic substance.

Young Paul tells his mother he is lucky, and subsequent events certainly bear this out: anyone who is able to beat the odds at the races and consistently pick winners is indubitably lucky. What he really means by this, however, is that he *loves* his mother so much that he is sure he can put right whatever is wrong in their family, can provide whatever she needs. His final words to his mother—"Mother, did I ever tell you? I am lucky!" (*CSS*, 3:804)—are really a desperate, confused proclamation of his love.

This merging of the categories of real and supernatural I have been tracing is wonderfully appropriate to the underlying themes of the story. The story is about a family whose parents are so confused about their own values, about the relative importance of love and money— that is, about what is *real*—that they destroy their family. The mother is pathetically superficial, but even she has a capacity for love. Unfortunately, she does not have the insight or the faith to value and cultivate love. The father too is so confused about what is important that he cannot find his own values, much less help his wife or children find their way through the dark wood of contemporary valuelessness.

In this situation the responsibility for setting the family right, for providing what it thinks it needs, falls to the son, a boy so young he should be occupied with nothing more serious or momentous than riding his rocking horse. He is called upon to tap into his natural store of love to try to put right the terrible unhappiness and confusion of values that he and his siblings sense in their family. Given the terrible "unnatural" burden this places on him, his uncle is doubtless right when he says, "poor devil, poor devil, he's best gone out of a life where he rides his rocking-horse to find a winner" (*CSS*, 3:804).

If reading this story produces occasional shivers on the back of our neck, it is not because of its ghostly quality, but rather because of the strange intersection of "natural" and "supernatural" with which it confronts us, disturbing us by calling into question the validity, the sufficiency, of our own self-knowledge, or our knowledge of the human psyche, our sense of what is real.

"The Woman Who Rode Away"

Fine short stories, even those in a realistic vein, always have ramifications beyond their specific characters and events. Hemingway's "Soldier's Home" is not simply about Kreb's difficulty in talking with his mother, but about the disorientation and desuetude that accompany the return to "normalcy" after events that have changed someone forever. Joyce's "The Dead" is not simply about a Twelfth-night afterdinner speech and a frustrated sexual opportunity, but about the assets and liabilities of self-awareness and concern for the integrity of one's "identity." "England, My England," as we have seen, is not simply about the self-disavowal of an overly sensitive person, but about a rivalry between life modes being played out in contemporary British culture and even in Western culture more broadly.

While many of Lawrence's stories undoubtedly do have social and cultural implications, his later "fabulistic" stories are distinguished from his more realistic and psychological earlier stories in the degree to which they are not simply about relationships among individuals but about larger cultural processes. This is certainly the case with "The Woman Who Rode Away," which has proved to be one of Lawrence's most controversial and misunderstood stories, largely because its distinctive nature and purpose have not been credited.[84] While some critics have praised the story as one of Lawrence's best and richest, others, including some admirers of Lawrence, have seen in it Lawrence at his worst.[85]

I have already spoken of the different kinds of demands involved in Lawrence's stories that are not structured around the development of individual relationships. In approaching this admittedly unpleasant, disturbing story I must stress that it is not simply a psychological study of a woman disappointed with what her life has become: it is about two processes of devolution, one individual, the other cultural, that reinforce one another. And this story is at least as much about the cultural process as the individual.[86]

A second point we must recognize—one that should not need saying, but obviously does—is that Lawrence does not approve of the events he is depicting here, in regard either to the woman or the Indians: the story will be badly misunderstood if it is viewed as Lawrence's mean-spirited attempt to vent his spleen against women or primitives.[87] It should be obvious that any writer concerned about the welfare and fate of his culture may have to write about subjects he himself finds deeply disturbing.

The rise and fall of cultures is a historical-psychic process that is just as real as the process of individuation or the development of a relationship between individuals. Cultures come into being and pass away, flourish and wither, and cultures like individuals can even lose faith in themselves. Such cultural processes are not easy to think about, both because of their scope and because the modern Western mind-set is so strangely naive about and resistant to such matters. We do especially need to think about such cultural processes nowadays because we are so reluctant to acknowledge the larger processes of history that effect the rise and fall of whole cultures or whole peoples, such as the American Indians.[88]

Such a large-scale process as the decline of a culture is admittedly an ambitious topic to take on within a short story—not even the longest novel could deal *comprehensively* with it—but Lawrence takes it on, and (I believe) succeeds, by virtue of his choosing with great care the situation of his story. What makes this story compelling is that the woman at the end of her personal tether and the Indians at the end of their cultural one, seek one another out for terrible, but perhaps predictable, uses. Each of them looks to the other for "salvation" in a way that expresses the desperation and futility of their situation.

For all its mythic elements the story does have a strong, persistent, realistic and psychological dimension, and if we are to understand what Lawrence is getting at here, we must begin by looking carefully, realistically, at the situations of both the woman and the Indians. The situation of the woman—who is identified only by her husband's name as Mrs. Lederman—is of course abominable: she is married to a man who embodies the worst faults of modern Western achievement, who regards her as property, and who sees his marriage as "the last and most intimate bit of his own works" (*CSS*, 2:547). But her problems began even before she knew her husband.

It is no accident that her place of origin is Berkeley, California, an intellectual colony on the far edge of Western culture. By the time of her marriage, she was already so saturated with her own individualistic life mode that she was looking for something utterly different, so she chose a man of strange circumstances in hopes that her marriage would be an "adventure" (*CSS*, 2:546). But in so doing she overreached herself, for her marriage has had no meaning for her; on the contrary, we are told, "Her conscious development had stopped mysteriously with her marriage, completely arrested. Her husband had never become real to her, neither mentally nor physically" (*CSS*, 2:547), and her eldest boy was nearly 10 years old before she "aroused from her stupor of subjected amazement" (*CSS*, 2:547), at age 33—an age propitious for apocalyptic events. From its opening pages the story depicts a woman whose life is a hollow frustration from which she wants badly to escape.

That the woman is desperately romantic is indicated in a variety of ways—for example, she responds strongly to the mining engineer's speculations about the "wonderful" quality of the "mysteries" that must exist in the hills and mountains, in spite of her husband's deflating characterization of the savages as dirty, unsanitary, and merely cunning (*CSS*, 2:549). And Lawrence is quite explicit about the woman's baseless romanticism in response to the engineer's speculations: "And this particular vague enthusiasm for unknown Indians found a full echo in the woman's heart. She was overcome by a foolish romanticism more unreal than a girl's. She felt it was her destiny to wander into the secret haunts of these timeless, mysterious, marvellous Indians of the mountains" (*CSS*, 2:549). Quite obviously, then, we are not asked to approve or condone the woman's romanticism or her desperate act in riding away to find the Indians. Rather, we are expected to see her act as the result of desperation prompted by her sense that she had reached the end of her tether. While we may sympathize with the woman, it should be clear that she is ripe for some extreme reaction against the utter nullity of her life. She is, then, hardly to be taken as a "paradigm" character—except in her representation of the frightening culmination of something in Western culture.

Other details confirm the interpretation that the woman's journey to the Indians is grounded in romanticism and escapism. When she first encounters the Indians, they are by no means wild or romantic; she notes that except for their long hair—which she reacts to with "a certain distaste"—"they would have been the same as the men who worked for her husband," and she thinks, "These must be the wild Indians she had come to see," also noting of one that "he did not look as if he had washed lately" (*CSS*, 2:553). Similarly, when they reach the village and look down on it from above, the "magic" of it is deflated by the statement, "There it was, all small and perfect, looking magical, as any place will look magical, seen from the mountains above" (*CSS*, 2:559).

Though we are told little about how Mrs. Lederman has come to her present state—much less than about Egbert, in "England, My England"—it is clear she wishes to escape and disavow her own will, her own individualism. Several times during her journey she wishes for and tries to convince herself of her own "death" (*CSS*, 2:552, 555, 556, 557), by which she means an obliteration of her personal self, her personal consciousness. But she never quite succeeds, for her will revives in spite of herself, and continues to do so even after she has been kept captive by the Indians for some months (see her questions and her challenges to the young Indian, *CSS*, 2:574–75).

Nor can she grasp the degree to which the Indians regard her *impersonally*, for she continues to project upon them an interest in her as a woman, a sexual interest, and is incredulous when they regard her indifferently, asexually (*CSS*, 2:557, 557–58, 560). Her "confidence in her own female power" (*CSS*, 2:554) also shows her inability to comprehend the Indians' perspective. Trying to resort to her "femaleness" as a source of power, she does not realize that the Indians' interests are far more generic, even cosmic, than in her "female power." If the Indians were to use such a term, they would mean by it something different than she. For her, it necessarily involves some power stemming from sexual *desire*, but for them her "female power" would involve her relationship with the moon. Much later, after spending some months with the Indians, she gains a clearer sense of what she regards as her apotheosis:

> Her kind of womanhood, intensely personal and individual, was to be obliterated again, and the great primeval symbols were to tower once more over the fallen individual independence of woman. The sharpness and the quivering nervous consciousness of the highly-bred white woman was to be destroyed again, womanhood was to be cast once more into the great stream of impersonal sex and impersonal passion. (*CSS*, 2:569)[89]

But we should note that her reaction to this is not exultation; rather, "she went back to her little house in a trace of agony."

In spite of having occasional glimpses of the death of her mode of consciousness—glimpses from which she always retreats—the woman finds no meaningful alternative to the dead end of her individualism in the rituals or myths of the Indians. There are several passages describing her sense of a different "state of consciousness" (*CSS*, 2:565, 568, 572, 573, 574), but we should not romanticize or be misled by these. These states are obviously drug-induced, and while they involve sensations other than those to which she is accustomed, they do not involve a new mode of consciousness for her. A truly different mode of consciousness is not so easily achieved.[90]

The first such passages focus upon heightened *sensations* that are the result of drug use (*CSS*, 2:565, 568, 572), and the language describing these states is by no means entirely positive. We are told, for example,

> She felt always in the same relaxed, *confused, victimized* state, unless the sweetened herb drink would *numb her mind altogether*, and release her senses into a sort of heightened, mystic acuteness and a

feeling as if she were diffusing out deliciously into the harmony of
things. This at length became the only state of consciousness that
she recognized: this exquisite sense of bleeding out into the higher
beauty and harmony of things. (*CSS*, 2:572; my emphasis)

This is not a new mode of consciousness taking the place of her received Western mode; it is drug-induced escapism that would be temporary if it were not continually forced upon her by Indians. (Some of
us have felt something similar from nitrous oxide, but it did not in fact
transform our psyche—we were back at work within a few hours.) Nor
should we be misled about the Indians' motives in all this: they are
not concerned about initiating the woman into the unique beauties of
their own worldview (which would presumably involve not constant
drugging, but teaching her their language, having her participate in
their rituals, and so forth), but simply to keep her quiescent until December 21. The woman does become virtually addicted to the effects
of the drug and comes even to welcome it: "Presently they gave her a
drink from a cup, which she took gladly, because of the semi-trance it
would induce" (*CSS*, 2:576). But even after the most rhapsodic account of its effects on her (573–74), we are told that "she had gone
into that other state of passional cosmic consciousness *like one who is
drugged*. The Indians, with there [*sic*] heavily religious natures, had
made her succumb to their vision" (*CSS*, 2:574; my emphasis). But it remains their vision, not hers. In short, it violates the persistent underlying realism of the story to claim this woman has found any meaningful
alternative to Western individualism.

Equally important to Lawrence's purposes in this story is the decline of the Indian culture, its loss of faith in the power of its traditional ways, and its coming to blame the white man (or woman) for
what has gone wrong. Since the story is presented from the woman's
perspective, this decline is not immediately obvious, for she is often
puzzled by what she sees, and much of the time she is drugged. But
the Indians' loss of faith in their culture and their resentment toward
the white race become obvious. When the woman first begins to question the young Indian, who has himself been sent far off into the
white man's world *because* he is to be the cacique (*CSS*, 2:567), he tells
her "we say, when a white woman sacrifice herself to our gods, then
our gods will *begin* to make the world *again*, and *the white man's gods will
begin to fall to pieces*" (*CSS*, 2:570; my emphasis).

A few paragraphs later, when the woman asks pointedly why the Indians are not masters of the white men, the Indian responds explicitly, "Because . . . the Indian got weak, and lost his power with the sun" (*CSS*, 2:571). Their discussion ends with the following exchange:

> "But," she faltered, "why do you hate us so? Why do you hate me?"
> He looked up suddenly with a light on his face, and a startling flame of a smile.
> "No, we don't hate," he said softly, looking with a curious glitter into her face.
> "You do," she said, forlorn and hopeless.
> And after a moment's silence, he rose and went away. (*CSS*, 2:571–72)

A few pages later it becomes obvious the Indians do blame the white race—more specifically the white woman—for what has gone wrong in their culture, and he admits "the sun is angry" (*CSS*, 2:575; the following paragraph specifically blames the white woman and characterizes her as "wicked"). And in response to the woman's sensible (personal) observation that "I don't shut out the moon—how can I?" she feels an unrelenting, impersonal hatred (*CSS*, 2:576).

All of these statements clearly show both that the Indians have felt some lapse in their powers, and that they believe the white race is somehow responsible for it. But it is by no means clear how or why a tribe so ancient and so isolated should be so affected by the white race. Certainly there is no evidence of actual depredation or disease, and so the Indians' blaming the white race seems a rationalization of a decline that stems from other sources.

Just as the woman embodies the end of the road of a kind of Western individualism, the Indian tribe embodies a devolution and turning back upon itself of their culture. This tribe has lost faith in the power of its beliefs and traditions, and has come to accept the idea that the source of their troubles is the white man, who has somehow appropriated their traditional sources of power. The woman's intentionally vague answers to their questions, and especially her admission that she is tired of the white man's god, inadvertently feeds into the Indians' wish to appropriate the power of the white man. This is explicitly indicated by the young Indian's statement that "We know the sun, and we know the moon. And we say, when a white woman sacrifice herself to our gods, then our gods will begin to make the world again, and the white man's gods will fall to pieces" (*CSS*, 2:570).

The story does not concern itself with the precise historical processes that have led up to the decline of this culture, whether external or internal, physical or spiritual. In any event, having now made contact with Western culture, they have (as Egbert did) come to disavow the value of their own traditional modes, in favor of the obvious power wielded by the white man, who has now become their standard, their criterion of power. Lawrence thus shows us that a culture as well as an individual can resort to desperate devices and rationalizations during its decline.

Several critics have observed the beauty and the poetic power of the descriptions of the natives' religious beliefs. This is quite true; these passages show us the wonderfully metaphoric, empathetic means by which the Indians express their understanding of the world around them, even of their own loss of power, which they have interpreted in terms of their myths. But the story shows clearly that while they can still articulate the traditional poetry of their tribe and still perform rituals involving the sun and the moon, they have lost faith in them; they are themselves no longer in living, meaningful rapport with the powers they invoke; and worst of all, they now look to a culture outside their own as both the cause of their problems and the source of their possible renewal—a culture so utterly different from their own that there can be no meaningful appropriation of its very different modes of power. That the Indians have lost their living faith in the religious attitudes evoked so convincingly by Lawrence renders these passages terribly poignant. (This corresponds, of course, to the woman's looking to something utterly foreign to her own background and traditions as a source of renewed meaning for her life.)[91]

That the process of cultural devolution Lawrence is exploring will be repeated many times in the history of our planet is suggested by an allusion that occurs within the woman's reflections. We are told, "In the strange towering symbols on the heads of the changeless, absorbed women she seemed to read once more the Mene Mene Tekel Upharsin. Her kind of womanhood, intensely personal and individual, was to be obliterated again, and the great primeval symbols were to tower once more over the fallen individual independence of woman" (*CSS*, 2:569). We should recall the biblical context of the allusion. Daniel interprets these words for King Belshazzar: "God hath numbered the days of your kingdom and brought it to an end; you have been weighed in the balances and found wanting; your kingdom is divided and given to the Medes and the Persians" (Daniel 5: 26–28), and we are told that that night Belshazzar the king of the Chaldeans was slain.

We moderns are of course aware that in the past kingdoms and cultures have risen and fallen, but we seem to feel our present-day self-awareness and knowledge and technology can forestall any such decline in our own culture. Moreover, some among us seem even to believe it possible to reverse the effects of one such recent cultural decline that is very close to that explored in the story: the erosion and virtual death of American Indian culture in the face of the Westward movement and the influences of modern American culture.

There are cultural processes of rise and fall that are no less tangible than the smaller scale, more observable individual processes. And just as it would be terrible to be an individual who for whatever reasons has given up on himself or herself—such as Egbert or Mrs. Lederman—it would be terrible as well to be a part of a culture that was waning and that had to resort to desperate acts to try to revive itself.

There is a frightening irony in the situation of the story: both this exhausted woman and this exhausted culture think they can find their salvation in the other. But the story shows clearly that she finds no such salvation, and it should be just as obvious that the sacrificial offering of the white woman will effect no change in the culture of the Chilchuis. Shortly before the sacrifice the woman reads in the faces of the Indians "The immense fundamental sadness, the grimness of ultimate decision, the fixity of revenge, and the nascent exultance of those that are going to triumph" (*CSS*, 2:577). The penultimate paragraph, reflecting the perspective of the old cacique, implies his confidence that his killing the woman will achieve something, but we, in our larger knowledge of the historical processes inexorably at work in the twentieth century, know what is actually in store for a small tribe of Central American Indians.[92]

The incomplete sentence that comprises the last paragraph is terrible in its implication: "The mastery that man must hold, and that passes from race to race." In this laconic statement Lawrence testifies to the need of each race, each people, to see their local habitation as the *axis mundi*, the *Omphalos*, the center of the world, but testifies as well to the inevitable ebb and flow of the larger processes of history.

For those who find themselves in a waning culture, as that of the Indians is and as our own some day will be, there is nothing within their power that will reverse the process.[93]

This story is admittedly unpleasant and depressing. None of the characters evokes approbation, and the final scene of human sacrifice is ghastly and revolting. But the serious artist must write about the concerns and problems of his culture, and so he cannot always depict characters or events that are admirable or enjoyable. And there is no doubt that degeneration, the drift toward death, whether of individuals or of a culture, is one of Lawrence's perennial themes. Several critics have assumed that because Lawrence has written so successfully, so evocatively, about these things, he must sanction them or approve of them in some way, so that finally the story expresses some misogyny on his part.

Why the central character must be a woman I cannot say, but certainly Lawrence used women as his psychic voyagers repeatedly throughout his career. I have noted above, he at this same time used other much more positive women to explore a situation similar to this one. Perhaps he felt that women were more sensitive to the debacle of modern Western culture in a way men were not—especially if that debacle involves elements such as those represented by Lederman in this story. In any event, we should not cut ourselves off from experiencing the terrible truths this story explores by the callow assumption that Lawrence sanctions what he is presenting.

In this dark, troubling story Lawrence juxtaposes two related questions. One is the question of what happens in the psyche of a culture in decline; this he explores through the Chilchuis, and he astutely shows how their response is shaped by the very myths they have always lived by. The other question is whether our own culture, represented by the woman, may not be verging toward overextension and collapse, and if so, how that process will work. We know Lawrence frequently explored the "drift toward death" in his works, both that of the individual and that of the culture—and often the one represents and epitomizes the other. This story is one of his darkest such explorations.

Notes to Part 1

1. F.R. Leavis makes the same point when he says that the "firsthandedness" of Lawrence's presentation makes demands that most critics are not

prepared to meet and has prevented his stories from being appropriately acclaimed; see his *D.H. Lawrence: Novelist* (New York: Alfred A. Knopf, 1956), 371–73. On the issue of the present attitude toward Lawrence, Keith Sagar has an interesting prefatory note to his "D.H. Lawrence: The Man and the Artist," in *The Modernists: Studies in a Literary Phenomenon. Essays in Honor of Harry T. Moore*, ed. Lawrence B. Gamache and Ian S. MacNiven (Rutherford, N.J.: Fairleigh Dickinson University Press, 1987), 114–25. Sagar says that he had earlier assumed that Lawrence was now fully recognized and accepted, but he has learned that he was wrong, and that Lawrence does still need fervent defenders.

2. Mark Schorer, "Technique as Discovery," *Hudson Review* 1 (1948): 67–87; hereafter cited in the text.

3. See, for example, Keith Cushman, "The Achievement of *England, My England and Other Stories*," in *D. H. Lawrence: The Man Who Lived*, ed. Robert B. Partlow and Harry T. Moore (Carbondale: Southern Illinois University Press, 1980), 27–38.

4. Frank O'Connor, *The Lonely Voice* (Cleveland: World, 1963), 16. O'Connor also quotes Turgenev's statement that "We all came out from under Gogol's 'Overcoat'" (14).

5. Anglo-Irish literature also provides many fine examples of such tales, but there is no evidence that Lawrence read them. Nineteenth-century Irish masters of the tale include William Carleton and Sheridan LeFanu. Twentieth century exemplars include Seumas O'Kelly, whose "The Weaver's Grave" is a superb example of a rich, meandering unmodernist tale; Sean O'Faolain; Elizabeth Bowen—for example, her Lawrencean-feeling "Summer Night"; and more recently Benedict Kiely and James Plunkett.

6. Walter Allen, *The Short Story in English* (Oxford: Oxford University Press, 1981), 99.

7. T. O. Beachcroft, *The Modest Art: A Survey of the Short Story in English* (Oxford: Oxford University Press, 1968), 209. Ronald P. Draper concurs: "Lawrence seems never to have considered the short story seriously as a form" (*D. H. Lawrence* [New York: Twayne, 1964], 119).

8. J. D. Chambers, ed., *D. H. Lawrence: A Personal Record*, 2d ed. (New York: Barnes and Noble, 1965). The fullest account of Lawrence's reading is Rose Marie Burwell's "A Checklist of Lawrence's Reading," in *A D.H. Lawrence Handbook*, ed. Keith Sagar (New York: Barnes and Noble, 1982), 59–125.

9. See, for example, H. M. Daleski, "Lawrence and George Eliot: The Genesis of *The White Peacock*," in *D. H. Lawrence and Tradition*, ed. Jeffrey Meyers (Amherst: University of Massachusetts Press, 1985). Daleski says, "I believe that George Eliot was the major initial influence on Lawrence, and that he indeed found himself through her" (53), but discusses only Lawrence's first novel.

10. Keith Cushman, "The Young D. H. Lawrence and the Short Story," *Modern British Literature* 3 (1978): 101–12; hereafter cited in the text.

11. *The Letters of D. H. Lawrence,* vol. 1, *September 1901–May 1913,* ed. James T. Boulton (Cambridge: Cambridge University Press, 1979), 139–40; hereafter cited in the text.

12. J. A. Hobson, "The Task of Realism," *English Review* 3 (October 1909): 543–54.

13. From Moynahan's "Foreword" to *A Modern Lover and Other Stories* (New York: Ballantine Books, 1969), xv.

14. The review is reprinted in *Phoenix: The Posthumous Papers of D. H. Lawrence,* ed. Edward D. McDonald (London: William Heinemann, 1936), 308–13—the quoted passage is on p. 313; hereafter cited in the text as *Phoenix.*

15. This preface can be found in *Phoenix II: Uncollected, Unpublished, and Other Prose Works by D. H. Lawrence,* ed. Warren Roberts and Harry T. Moore (New York: Viking Press, 1970), 279–88—the quoted passages are on p. 281; hereafter cited in the text as *Phoenix II.*

16. A. E. Coppard, *Collected Tales* (New York: Alfred A. Knopf, 1948), vii–viii.

17. The most famous and influential example of normative short story theory is Poe's 1842 review of Hawthorne's *Twice-Told Tales.* Another well-known instance is Brander Matthews's *The Philosophy of the Short-Story* (London: Longmans, Green, and Co., 1901), which had appeared in magazine format in 1884 and 1885. On discussion of the genre at the turn of the century, see chapter 1 of Valerie Shaw's *The Short Story: A Critical Introduction* (London: Longman, 1983).

18. A fine discussion of Lawrence's exploratory mode is Mark Kinkead-Weekes, "The Marble and the Statue: The Exploratory Imagination of D. H. Lawrence," in *Imagined Worlds: Essays on Some English Novels and Novelists in Honour of John Butt,* ed. Maynard Mack and Ian Gregor (London: Methuen and Co., 1968), 371–418.

19. *The Letters of D. H. Lawrence,* vol. 2, *June 1913–October 1916,* ed. George J. Zytaruk and James T. Boulton (Cambridge: Cambridge University Press, 1981), 90; hereafter cited in the text.

20. *Study of Thomas Hardy and Other Essays,* ed. Bruce Steele (Cambridge: Cambridge University Press, 1985), 172.

21. "Why the Novel Matters," in *Study of Thomas Hardy and Other Essays,* 195. See my discussion in the Headnote to Part 2.

22. *Letters,* 1: 491, 492. For other relevant letters see *Letters,* 1:330, 455, 470, 477. The letter to Edward Garnett of 19 November 1912 is particularly important. It contains Lawrence's defense of the form of *Sons and Lovers,* and Frieda's postscript defending Lawrence against the charge of formlessness, in which she says, "really he is the only revolutionary worthy of the name . . . any new thing must find a new shape, then afterwards one can call it 'art'" (*Letters,*

1:479). For a similar later statement on form—and disavowing authorial effacement—see Lawrence's letter to Carlo Linati of 22 January 1925 in *The Letters of D. H. Lawrence*, vol. 5, *March 1924–March 1927*, ed. James T. Boulton and Lindeth Vasey (Cambridge: Cambridge University Press, 1989), 200–201; hereafter cited in the text.

23. Lawrence's growth during this period has been the subject of several critical discussions. See, for example, Keith Cushman, *D. H. Lawrence at Work: The Emergence of the Prussian Officer Stories* (Charlottesville: University of Virginia Press, 1978); Brian H. Finney, "D. H. Lawrence's Progress to Maturity: From Holograph Manuscript to Final Publication of *The Prussian Officer and Other Stories*," *Studies in Bibliography* 28 (1975): 321–32; Janice Harris, *The Short Fiction of D. H. Lawrence* (New Brunswick, N.J.: Rutgers University Press, 1984) Passim; J.C.F. Littlewood, "D. H. Lawrence's Early Tales," *Cambridge Quarterly* 1 (1966): 107–24. See also the introductions to the Cambridge Press editions of *The Prussian Officer*, (1987), edited by David Farmer, Lindeth Vasey, and John Worthen, and of *The Rainbow* (1989), edited by Mark Kinkead-Weekes.

24. The influence of Balzac, for instance, is more substantial and lasting than that of Maupassant, involving not just technical facility but a whole attitude of sympathy toward a wide range of persons. Consider Lawrence's comment in a letter to Blanche Jennings of 11 November 1908: "Balzac can lay bare the living body of the great Life better than anybody in the world. He doesn't hesitate at the last covering; he doesn't point out all the absurdities of the intricate innumerable wrappings and accessories of the body of Life; he goes straight to the flesh; and, unlike de Maupassant or Zola, he doesn't inevitably light on a wound, or a festering sore" (*Letters*, 1:91–92).

25. Hardy's influence and the importance to Lawrence's development of his "Study of Thomas Hardy" have been discussed by several critics; see, for example, Ross C. Murfin, *Swinburne, Hardy, Lawrence and the Burden of Belief* (Chicago: University of Chicago Press, 1978); Michael Squires, *The Pastoral Novel: Studies in George Eliot, Thomas Hardy, and D. H. Lawrence* (Charlottesville: University of Virginia Press, 1974); Mark Kinkead-Weekes, "Lawrence on Hardy," in *Thomas Hardy After Fifty Years*, ed. Lance St. John Butler (Totowa, N.J.: Rowman and Littlefield, 1977), 90–103; Robert Langbaum, "Lawrence and Hardy," in *D. H. Lawrence and Tradition*, ed. Jeffrey Meyers (Amherst: University of Massachusetts Press, 1985); and Bruce Steele, "Introduction" to the Cambridge University Press edition of *Study of Thomas Hardy and Other Essays* (1985).

26. H. E. Bates, *The Modern Short Story* (London: Nelson and Sons, 1943), 203.

27. Elizabeth Bowen, "D. H. Lawrence: Reappraising His Literary Influence," *New York Times Book Review*, 9 February 1947, p. 4.

28. Philip Hobsbaum, *A Reader's Guide to D. H. Lawrence* (London: Thames and Hudson, 1981), 29–30; hereafter cited in the text.

29. Two recent collections of essays dealing with Lawrence's influence are *The Legacy of D. H. Lawrence: New Essays*, ed. Jeffrey Meyers (New York: St. Martin's Press, 1987), and *D. H. Lawrence's Literary Inheritors*, ed. Keith Cushman and Dennis Jackson (New York: St. Martin's Press, 1991). But the former, though organized by literary genre, has no essay specifically on Lawrence and the short story. The latter contains only two essays dealing with writers best known for their short fiction—Eudora Welty and Raymond Carver—and the essay on Carver presents his surprising claim that he had not read "The Blind Man" before writing his "Cathedral."

30. James Joyce explores this complex question of artistic transcendence through Stephen Dedalus's Shakespeare theory in *Ulysses*—the question of how a writer's works can come to terms with issues that are implicit within his life experience more wisely than the writer can do in his own person. Our detailed knowledge of the lives of twentieth-century writers provides unparalleled temptations to indulge in the biographical or genetic fallacy, but it should also provide us with opportunities to break out of it, by exploring fully the presumed biographical "sources" of various works.

31. Another critic who has condemned Lawrence for heavy-handed techniques, but now acknowledges the distinctiveness of Lawrence's methods is Wayne C. Booth. See his "Confessions of a Lukewarm Lawrentian," in *The Challenge of D. H. Lawrence*, ed. Michael Squires and Keith Cushman (Madison: University of Wisconsin Press, 1990), 9–27. Booth says, "Lawrence was experimenting radically with what it means for a novelist to lose his own distinct voice in the voices of his characters, especially in their inner voices. In his practice, all rules about point of view are abrogated: the borderlines between author's voice and character's voice are deliberately blurred, and only the criticism of the whole tale will offer any sort of clarity to the reader seeking to sort out opinions" (16).

32. James Joyce, *A Portrait of the Artist as a Young Man* (New York: Viking Press, 1964), 215. Stephen's phrase adapts ideas expressed by Flaubert in his letters: see *The Workshop of Daedalus: James Joyce and the Raw Materials for "A Portrait of the Artist as a Young Man,"* ed. Robert Scholes and Richard M. Kain (Evanston, Ill.: Northwestern University Press, 1965), 247–48.

33. "The Blind Man," in *England, My England*, ed. Bruce Steele (Cambridge: Cambridge University Press, 1990), 46; hereafter cited in the text as *EME*.

34. I borrow the device of illustrating the subtleties of attributed narration by restatement in the first person from Donald Ross, Jr.'s "Who's Talking? How Characters Become Narrators in Fiction" (*Modern Languages Notes* 91 [1976]: 1222–42).

35. The story was apparently written in May–June 1913. John Worthen cites evidence that this is the story Lawrence refers to in his letter to Edward Garnett of 10 June 1913; see Worthen's edition of *Love Among the Haystacks* (Cambridge: Cambridge University Press, 1987), xxxviii–xl. It seems unlikely

that this is one of the stories Lawrence revised in the summer of 1914, in preparation for the *Prussian Officer* volume. Worthen says, "Early in July [1914], Lawrence seriously considered it for *The Prussian Officer*, and on 2 July asked Douglas Clayton [the typist] 'I wonder if you have got, and if you could let me have at once, the MS. of "Love Among the Haystacks," and "The Old Adam and the New Eve," or a story with a title something like that' [*Letters*, 2:190]; but within a week, his conception of the volume had changed" (*Love Among the Haystacks*, xxxix; hereafter cited in the text as *LAH*). This story is not in the list of 12 stories for the new volume that he sent to Edward Garnett on 14 July 1914 (*Letters*, 2:197).

36. See his letter of 2 June 1914 to Arthur McLeod, in which he speaks of the need for "men to have courage to draw nearer to women, expose themselves to them, and be altered by them . . . gaining great blind knowledge and suffering and joy" (*Letters*, 2:181; quoted more fully below in Part 2). The letter of 23 April 1913 to Arthur McLeod (*Letters*, 1:543–44) speaks as well of the need for a readjustment between men and women, and a letter to Gordon Campbell of 21 September 1914 is eloquent on this same point (*Letters*, 2:218).

37. Donald Ross, "Who's Talking?" Ross cites the paragraph beginning "She went forward. . . ."; See *The Prussian Officer and Other Stories*, ed. John Worthen (Cambridge: Cambridge University Press, 1983), 125; hereafter cited in the text as *PO*.

38. Lawrence's exploration of inherently vague regions of the psyche has parallels in the thought of A. N. Whitehead and Michael Polanyi. Compare Whitehead's challenge to Hume's presupposition that what is clearest and most distinct in our thought is therefore most important ("Objects and Subjects," in *Adventures in Ideas* [New York: Macmillan, 1933]), and Polanyi's discussion of "subsidiary awareness" in *Personal Knowledge: Towards a Post-Critical Philosophy* (Chicago: University of Chicago Press, 1958; rev. ed. 1962).

39. Virginia Woolf, "Modern Fiction," in *Collected Essays*, vol. 2 (New York: Harcourt, Brace and World, 1967), 106.

40. In "Why the Novel Matters," Lawrence says, "I shall never know wherein lies my integrity, my individuality, my me. I *can* never know it. It is useless to talk about my ego. That only means that I have made up an *idea* of myself, and that I am trying to cut myself out to pattern. Which is no good. You can cut your cloth to fit your coat, but you can't clip bits off your living body, to trim it down to your idea. True, you can put yourself into ideal corsets. But even in ideal corsets, fashions change" (*Study of Thomas Hardy and Other Essays*, 197).

41. "Foreword to *Women in Love*," in *Women in Love* (Cambridge: Cambridge University Press, 1987), 486. For a fuller discussion of this topic see Thomas H. McCabe, "Rhythm as Form in Lawrence: 'The Horse-Dealer's Daughter,'" *PMLA* 87 (1972): 65–68.

42. In the first version of "The Spirit of Place" Lawrence says "Every people is polarised in some particular locality, some home or homeland. And

every great era of civilisation seems to be the expression of a particular continent or continent region, as well as of the people concerned," and later,
"Every great locality expresses itself perfectly, in its own flowers, its own
birds and beasts, and lastly its own men, with their perfected works" (*The Symbolic Meaning* [New York: Viking Press, 1964], 20, 30). This quality was recognized by the anonymous *New York Times Book Review* reviewer of *England, My
England*, who says of Lawrence "he has the ability, not merely to show us a
place, but to make us feel its spiritual atmosphere" (in *D. H. Lawrence: The
Critical Heritage*, ed. R. P. Draper [London: Routledge and Kegan Paul, 1979],
190). Aldous Huxley is indicating this same quality when he refers to landscape as the "background and the principal personage" of all Lawrence's novels, in his Introduction to *The Letters of D. H. Lawrence* (New York: Viking
Press, 1932), xxx.

43. Lawrence speaks directly to this point in "The Novel" when he says,
"And this is the beauty of the novel; everything is true in its own relationship,
and no further.... So, if a character in a novel wants two wives—or three—or
thirty: well, that is true of that man, at that time, in that circumstance. It may
be true of other men, elsewhere or elsewhen. But to infer that all men at all
times want two, three, or thirty wives; or that the novelist himself is advocating furious polygamy; is just imbecility" (*Study of Thomas Hardy and Other Essays*, 185).

44. In the first version of "The Spirit of Place" Lawrence pointedly says
that we find it easier to understand "the sending of wireless messages from
continent to continent" than to understand "that the unthinkably sensitive
substance of human intelligence could receive the fine waves of vital
effluence transmitted across the intervening space" (*The Symbolic Meaning*, 23).

45. The critical literature on this story is extensive. Critics who have
dealt specifically with the successive endings of the story include Keith Cushman, *Lawrence at Work* (1978); Mara Kalnins, "D. H. Lawrence's 'Odour of
Chrysanthemums': The Three Endings," reprinted in *Critical Essays on D. H.
Lawrence*, ed. Dennis Jackson and Fleda Brown Jackson, (Boston: G. K. Hall
and Co., 1988), 145–53; and James T. Boulton, "D. H. Lawrence's 'Odour of
Chrysanthemums': An Early Version," *Renaissance and Modern Studies* 13
(1969): 5–48.

46. For example, Frank Amon says of the story, "The revelation of
theme ... comes to the wife through the death of her husband. Revelation
through death is then the means of objectifying the theme. However, it is the
moment of revelation with which we are concerned here and with the peculiar
means of objectifying that moment" ("D. H. Lawrence and the Short Story,"
in *The Achievement of D. H. Lawrence*, ed. Frederick J. Hoffman and Harry T.
Moore (Norman: University of Oklahoma Press, 1953), 223–24; my emphasis).
Other critics who talk similarly of Elizabeth's epiphanic realization of the
truth include Keith Cushman, who uses the word *epiphany* (*Lawrence at Work*,
58) and Mara Kalnins (*Critical Essays*, 151).

47. Written late in 1909 and submitted to the *English Review* in December, the story was immediately accepted by Ford Madox Hueffer (according to the famous story) and was set in proof by March 1910. (Fortunately, a manuscript survives that presents the ending of a version dating from 1909—according to Worthen, *PO*, 1—printed as Appendix 1 of the Cambridge *Prussian Officer*.) But publication of the story was so long delayed that in March 1911 Lawrence extensively revised these page proofs before it appeared in the *English Review* in June 1911. In a letter of 2 April 1911, Lawrence wrote to Louie Burrows, "It has taken me such a long time to write those last two pages of the story. You have no idea how much delving it requires to get that deep into cause and effect" (*Letters*, 1:250). Before publication in the *Prussian Officer* volume in November 1914, Lawrence twice more revised the story—in July and in October 1914—both times rewriting the ending (Worthen, *PO*, li). Keith Cushman is undoubtedly right when he says, "The final tableau in 'Odour of Chrysanthemums' is absolutely central in Lawrence's experience" (*Lawrence at Work*, 55).

48. In support of his claim that the story turns upon Lawrence's realization of human isolation, Keith Cushman points to the passage in Chapter IX of *The Rainbow* where Lydia is viewing the laid-out body of Tom Brangwen, claiming "The marriage of Tom and Lydia Brangwen, like that of Walter and Elizabeth Bates, is a study in human isolation" (*Lawrence at Work*, 73). But while the relationship of Tom and Lydia was never articulate, it was a real, meaningful relationship. Interestingly, Mara Kalnins cites this same passage, but acknowledges the complexity of the Tom/Lydia relationship, quoting the passage about the "strange, inviolable completeness of the two of them" (*Rainbow*, 47, quoted by Kalnins, in *Critical Essays*, 151). Moreover, Kalnins asserts the striking similarity of the passage in "Odour" with Lydia's feelings not about Tom but about her first husband, Paul Lensky. She also cites analogous passages from other works, in which a character has a sense of the otherness of someone he or she is intimately involved with. But in all such scenes in Lawrence's works, the characters' categorical statements must be understood "contextually"—must be understood, that is, as expressing their feelings in that situation—and we should not elevate or hypostatize such statements into absolute truths.

49. Similarly, Mara Kalnins, though claiming for Elizabeth a "revelation . . . as she perceives and understands at last the meaning of death and of life," says that the writing here "mirrors the incoherent workings of a mind under emotional stress" (*Critical Essays*, 151), and she quotes Lawrence's own words: "How does one think when one is thinking passionately and with suffering? Not in words at all but in strange surges and cross-currents of emotion which are only half-rendered by words" (*The First Lady Chatterley* [New York: Dial Press, 1944], 194).

50. In Lawrence's works, statements such as "He saw suddenly . . ." or "At last he had learned," as in "The Shadow in the Rose Garden" (*PO*, 132),

are rarely to be trusted, for the character probably understands much less than he thinks he does. One of Lawrence's most persistent themes is the necessarily gradual assimilation of those life-truths that lie closest to us. Epiphanic, instantaneous understanding of anything meaningful implies a superficial, tabula rasa image of the mind very different from Lawrence's view of the human psyche.

51. In the final version Elizabeth's response to Walter's death is more emotionally controlled and coherent and less obviously involves evasions and idealizations. In the 1910 *English Review* proof version, she clearly does not want him to come back to life: "She did not want him to wake up, she did not want him to speak. She had him again, now, and it was Death which had brought him. She kissed him, so that she might kiss Death which had taken the ugly things from him.... She loved him so much now; her life was mended again, and her faith looked up with a smile; he had come home to her, beautiful. How she had loathed him! It was strange he could have been such as he had been. How wise of death to be so silent. If he spoke, even now, her anger and her scorn would lift their heads like fire. He would not speak—no, just gently smile, with wide eyes" (Boulton, 44).

52. See Keith Cushman, "D. H. Lawrence at Work: 'The Shadow in the Rose Garden,'" *D. H. Lawrence Review* 8 (1975): 31–46. His article deals with three versions of the story created between 1908 and autumn 1914. Brian Finney also discusses the three versions in his "D. H. Lawrence's Progress to Maturity: From Holograph Manuscript to Final Publication of *The Prussian Officer and Other Stories,*" *Studies in Bibliography* 28 (1975): 321–32, arguing that the 1914 version differs little in plot from that of 1913, but "excavates deeper into the characters' less conscious feelings" (327). John Worthen dates the writing of "The Vicar's Garden" to autumn 1907 and says that perhaps the story was reworked in the spring of 1911 (*D. H. Lawrence: The Early Years, 1885–1912* [Cambridge: Cambridge University Press, 1991], 472, 300).

53. In his *Philosophy of the Short-story* Brander Matthews quotes a letter from Robert Louis Stevenson saying, "Make another end to it? Ah, yes, but that's not the way I write; the whole tale is implied; I never use an effect when I can help it unless it prepares the effects that are to follow; that's what a story consists in. To make another end, that is to make the beginning all wrong. The *dénouement* of a long story is nothing, it is just 'a full close,' which you may approach and accompany as you please—it is a coda, not an essential member in the rhythm; but the body and end of a short-story is bone of the bone and blood of the blood of the beginning" (15–16; Matthews cites Stevenson's *Valima Letters,* 1:147).

54. The events and chronology of the story, though vague, are relevant to its meaning and deserve attention—especially since more than one critic has misread them. Kingsley Widmer says that this is the "first day of marriage" (*The Art of Perversity: D. H. Lawrence's Shorter Fictions* [Seattle: University of Washington Press, 1962], 154; hereafter cited in the text). Cushman

says that the earliest version involves a honeymooning couple. In fact, the couple talks of the *prospect* of a honeymoon. In the *Prussian Officer* version, the relationship between the young woman and the vicar's son is now several years in the past. The two met when she was 23 and he 26, which was some five or six years in the past (*PO*, 131). The young woman lived in this town for two years (*PO*, 122), she met the young vicar's son only two months after she went to work for Miss Birch (*PO*, 132), and they were "engaged" for nearly a year before the young man "suddenly went out to fight in Africa" (*PO*, 131). Since some time must have elapsed between their meeting and their "engagement," the young woman cannot have stayed on in the town very long after his departure, if she lived there only two years. She must have left the village soon after his departure for Africa, for clearly she was gone by the time Miss Birch told her of the sunstroke and death of the vicar's son, which must have been about four years earlier. She met Frank "almost the very day" (*PO*, 131) that she heard about the sunstroke, suggesting perhaps a relationship on the rebound. Clearly they have known one another for several years, and seem to have been married for some time.

55. Important temperamental differences between the wife and the husband are suggested by their different gardens and by the uses they make of them. Early in the story the young husband walks out into the cottage garden: "He contemplated the Tree of Heaven that flourished by the lawn, then sauntered on to the next plant. There was more promise in a crooked apple tree covered with red-brown fruit." Sampling its fruit, he finds "To his surprise the fruit was sweet" (*PO*, 121). Given his pragmatic disdain of the ideal and willingness to try its imperfect fruit, his garden becomes a source of pleasure; hers, for all its beauty, is a would-be sanctum and thus deathly.

56. The woman's slowly absorbed response illustrates the insufficiency of the "epiphanic" notion of human understanding—a theme discussed in my analysis of "Odour of Chrysanthemums."

57. Recall what Lawrence says in "We Need One Another": "We all want to be absolute, and sufficient unto ourselves. And it is a great blow to our self-esteem that we simply *need* another human being" (*Phoenix*, 188). And in "Morality and the Novel": "Each time we strive to a new relation, with anyone or anything, it is bound to hurt somewhat. Because it means the struggle with and the displacing of old connections, and this is never pleasant. And, moreover, between living things at least, an adjustment means also a fight; for each party, inevitably, must 'seek its own' in the other, and be denied" (*Study of Thomas Hardy and Other Essays*, 174).

58. Critical opinion is divided on the young couple's prospects. Kingsley Widmer predictably reads it negatively (*Art of Perversity*, 156), as does Keith Cushman ("Lawrence at Work," *D. H. Lawrence Review*, 44). Brian Finney is more positive: "In the violent release of hatred on both sides, the wife is finally forced to recognize the strength of her husband's personality, while he is made to acknowledge the gulf separating them" ("Lawrence's Progress

to Maturity," 328). Janice Harris says that they "have been shocked out of their blindness by having their sense of themselves and their world attacked ... the story avoids neat closure. It is enough that eyes have been opened, that the stream of conscience has been undammed" (*Short Fiction of D. H. Lawrence*, 103).

59. Critics who make this assumption include Graham Hough, *The Dark Sun: A Study of D. H. Lawrence* (London: Duckworth, 1956), 172–73; Emile Delavenay, *D. H. Lawrence: The Man and His Work. The Formative Years, 1885–1919* (London: William Heinemann, 1972), 431–34; and Harry T. Moore, *The Priest of Love: A Life of D. H. Lawrence*, rev. ed. (New York: Farrar, Straus, and Giroux, 1974), who dismisses the story as Lawrence's "cruelest story a clef"(270). But see the disclaimer by Barbara Lucas (daughter of Madeleine and Percy Lucas) in "Apropos of 'England, My England'" (*Twentieth Century* 169 [March 1961]: 288–93), who refutes the idea that Percy was the model for Egbert. In his *D. H. Lawrence: The Man and His Works* (Toronto: Forum House, 1969), Moore says even more simplistically, "The central figure of the story is a portrait of E. V. Lucas's younger brother, Percy" (174). Kingsley Widmer in *The Art of Perversity* resorts too easily to a "deeper nihilism and a longing for death" to explain Egbert's decline (17–22). John B. Vickery discusses the story in *Myths and Texts: Strategies of Incorporation and Displacement* (Baton Rouge: Louisiana State University Press, 1983), 38–45. Interesting as it is, Vickery's mythic approach causes him to neglect just those psychological aspects that I focus upon. Charles Rossman's "Myth and Misunderstanding D. H. Lawrence," in *Twentieth-Century Poetry, Fiction, Theory*, ed. Harry T. Garvin (Lewisburg, Pa.: Bucknell University Press, 1977), 81–101, is to some extent a rejoinder to Vickery.

60. F. R. Leavis says that the "theme of the tale is the impossibility of making a life with no more than this," and of Egbert he judges, "He stood, says Lawrence, 'for nothing.' He is irresponsible, ineffective, and, in his 'independent' way, parasitic" (*D. H. Lawrence: Novelist*, 333, 335).

61. Alastair Niven says (more truly than he realizes), "Lawrence probably asks too much if he intends us to read the whole plight of this class [English gentility] into one short story" (*D. H. Lawrence: The Writer and His Work* [New York: Charles Scribner's Sons, 1980], 84).

62. In approaching the story in terms of these radically complementary types, I am reminded of a statement by Jose Ortega y Gasset: "For there is no doubt that the most radical division that it is possible to make of humanity is that which splits it into two classes of creature; those who make great demands on themselves, piling up difficulties and duties; and those who demand nothing special of themselves, but for whom to live is to be every moment what they already are, without imposing on themselves any efforts towards perfection; mere buoys that float on the waves" (*The Revolt of the Masses* [New York: W. W. Norton, 1932], 15).

63. In the Cambridge *EME* text the story comprises pages 5–33, the flashback pages 5–18.

64. An interesting sidelight on the opportunity Egbert brings to Winifred is provided by Winifred's mother (who is not a Marshall by blood): "Her mother once said to her, with that characteristic touch of irony: 'Well, dear, if it is your fate to consider the lilies, that toil not, neither do they spin, that is one destiny among many others, and perhaps not so unpleasant as most. Why do you take it amiss, my child?'" (*EME*, 12). Nor should we be surprised to learn that "The mother was subtler than her children, they very rarely knew how to answer her. So Winifred was only more confused."

65. In any event, it is described much less fully here than in the October 1915 *English Review* version, in which 10 of the story's 15 pages are devoted to this denouement; see the appendix to the Cambridge edition of *EME*, 217–32.

66. "The Blind Man" was written in the summer and autumn of 1918, and appeared almost simultaneously in the *English Review* (July 1920) and in *Living Age* (7 August 1920). The version that appears in *EME* differs hardly at all from that in the periodicals (see the Cambridge *EME*, xxxv–xxxvi and 260–61, for details).

67. The relationship of Ursula and Birkin at the end of *Women in Love* is similar, with Birkin acknowledging the need of something beyond the marriage, and Ursula puzzled and frustrated as to why she cannot provide all that he needs.

68. A similar situation exists with George and Meg in *The White Peacock*, where she feels no need of the friends that George invites. George complains, "Nobody comes here to see me twice," he said "Because Meg receives them in such an off-hand fashion. I asked Jim Curtiss and his wife from Everley Hall one evening. We were uncomfortable all the time. Meg had hardly a word for anybody—'Yes' and 'No' and 'Hm Hm!'—They'll never come again" (*The White Peacock*, ed. Andrew Robertson [Cambridge: Cambridge University Press, 1983], 297).

69. Written in January 1919, the story was first published in the *Metropolitan* magazine in New York in August 1921, and subsequently in a collection called *The New Decameron III* (1922)—items B10 and C84 in Warren Roberts's *Bibliography*. See Bruce Steele's notes in the Cambridge *EME*, xxxvii–xli.

70. Of the few brief discussions of the story, none has felt this issue worth attending to. Tedlock notes the anomaly among the rather objective stories of *England, My England* of the use of an observer-narrator, but presumes the validity of the narrator's perspective (*D. H. Lawrence: Artist and Rebel*, 112). Janice Harris says pointedly that Lawrence's use of the first-person convention here "does not limit or expand his usual voice because the tale

is not about the narrator or anyone in particular" (*Short Fiction of D. H. Lawrence*, 148). Kingsley Widmer does not even take note of the mode of presentation of the tale, and consequently accepts the characterization of Maggie as a witch, referring to her as the "witch wife" and the "female witch" (*Art of Perversity*, 110, 111). Dismissal of the story's point of view causes these critics to read the story, in Harris's phrase as "shallowly misogynistic" (*Short Fiction of D. H. Lawrence*, 281)—a view shared by Tedlock and Widmer.

71. The peacocks—and especially Joey, whom Maggie brought with her from her home—are used by Maggie as an object of affection and attention. In the bird's capacity to "recoil inside himself inexplicably" (*EME*, 84), and his "inscrutable" quality (*EME*, 85), he mirrors for the narrator—and perhaps for Alfred as well—Maggie's own ability to be self-contained and untouchable. Silly as it is for Alfred to be jealous of the peacock, he obviously is.

72. Lawrence rewrote much of this final scene, from *EME* 88.39 through 90.33. The manuscript version shows more antagonism between the men, the revised version more enjoyment by the narrator of Alfred's vulnerable position. The most important change is in regard to Alfred's statement about his wife. In the manuscript he says "I don't love that hell-cat up yonder" (*EME*, 244), which is replaced by "She's a little devil, she is. But I shall have it out with her" (*EME*, 90).

73. Bruce Steele explains that "nothing is known of the genesis of this story," but suggests that it probably dates from late June or July 1919 (*EME*, xli). It was published in *Land and Water* on 29 April 1920. No manuscript or typescript survives.

74. The story has been discussed by several critics, but their discussions usually pursue one of the false trails that the story inadvertently provides, involving social class or male dominance or certain of Lawrence's presumed pet peeves. Janice Harris, for example, sees this story (as "The Fox") as clearly advocating the idea that the male should lead, but then she goes on to point out all the quite obviously bad qualities of the male characters (*Short Fiction of D. H. Lawrence*, 152). And Keith Cushman sees the story as downright negative saying, "A story which seems to be presenting the power of physical attraction is actually once again illustrating the fundamental hostility between men and women" ("Achievement of *England, My England*," 35). Certainly the story depicts some effects of social class, male attempts at dominance, and the like, but to regard it as *about* these issues misses the thrust of a wonderful story that dramatizes human needs struggling for expression in spite of a variety of impediments.

75. The *Land and Water* version is even more explicit about the poor prospects of marriage for women such as Matilda and Emily; for two sentences that Lawrence deleted, see *EME*, 266.

76. Judith Ruderman deals with an extensive array of predatory females in her *D. H. Lawrence and the Devouring Mother* (Durham, N.C.: Duke University Press, 1984). Ruderman reads this story, however, very differently than I,

seeing the "important relationship" as that "between the two men, rather than between the man and the woman" (82), and claiming that "revenge upon Matilda for her mothering of him and a desire for control over the homeplace motivate Hadrian's proposal of marriage" (83).

77. Apparently written in May 1926, "Two Blue Birds" appeared in the *Dial* in April 1927 and in *Pall Mall* in June 1928. It was first collected in *Great Stories of All Nations* (1927; see Roberts's *Bibliography*, item B22), before appearing in *The Woman Who Rode Away and Other Stories* in 1928.

78. The elusiveness of the story's perspective, and the perils of categorizing Lawrence's stories, is shown by Julian Moynahan's decision to include "Two Blue Birds" among what he calls "one of the most clear-cut groups among Lawrence's stories," a group "united by their rather bitchy, facetious tone" (*The Deed of Life: The Novels and Tales of D. H. Lawrence* [Princeton: Princeton University Press, 1963], 179). By categorizing it so superficially, Moynahan—usually a sympathetic and perceptive reader of Lawrence—cuts himself off from experiencing the distinctive qualities of this wonderful story. K. Widmer takes the woman at her word and so regards her utterly unsympathetically as a "type of self-sufficient woman" who "wants expensive clothes, travel, lovers, and all the rest of the 'vehement pursuit of enjoyment'" (*Art of Perversity*, 107).

79. F. R. Leavis makes the same point when, in his discussion of this story, he says that Lawrence's "presentations of individual lives have such force because they are at the same time, and inseparably, studies of the societies to which the individuals belong" (*D. H. Lawrence: Novelist*, 355).

80. The story was written in February 1926 and sent to Lady Cynthia Asquith in place of "Glad Ghosts," which was considered unsuitable for the volume of ghost stories she was compiling. A letter to Lady Cynthia dated 15 April 1926 suggests that the story was written for her volume: "I'm glad that you liked the 'Rocking-Horse': I told Miss Pearn to agree with you for terms and all that. After all, I wrote the story for you, not the magazines" (*Letters*, 5:424; Nancy Pearn was manager of the magazine department of Curtis Brown, London). The story's first publication, however, was in *Harper's Bazaar*, July 1926. In a letter of 25 February 1926 to Nancy Pearn, Lawrence asks her to send it to Lady Cynthia, saying, "It will perhaps be more suitable, and *spectral enough*" (*Letters*, 5:400; my emphasis).

81. Eudora Welty has commented on Lawrence's wonderful indifference to the everyday world, to realism, in his short stories generally. See her comments reprinted in "The Critics."

82. Surprising among the generally laudatory criticism on this story is the negative judgment of two respected critics of Lawrence. In his *D. H. Lawrence: Novelist*, F. R. Leavis refers to it as a "minor thing," and expresses his exasperation "to find it so widely regarded (especially in America, it would seem) as representative of the Lawrentian short story"(371). Graham Hough says it "is not at all a Laurencean story," and that "the supernatural element is boldly

and properly left unexplained, and is not made the substitute for a psychological reality that could be presented without it. The theme develops into a hectic and pathetic tale of gambling fever that destroys the boy himself as it reaches a successful climax; most skillfully done, but quite outside the range of Lawrence's usual work" (*Dark Sun*, 188). The explanation of this puzzling insensitivity to the quality of one of Lawrence's finest stories must lie in Lawrence's willingness to blatantly merge what are usually regarded as different "categories" of story—the realistic social/familial tale, and the supernatural. Thus these critics cannot recognize its kinship with other Lawrence stories.

83. Consider the statement that Lawrence made in a letter written many years before this story—coincidentally, to Lady Cynthia Asquith: "We are here with my sister, and two children—a very delightful boy of three, and a girl of seven. I am surprised how children are like barometers to their parents' feelings. There is some sort of queer, magnetic psychic connection—something a bit fatal, I believe. . . . The phenomenon of motherhood, in these days, is a strange and rather frightening phenomenon" (*Letters*, 3:245; 3 June 1918).

84. The story was written in the summer of 1924, in close conjunction with *St. Mawr*, and soon followed by "The Princess." Janice Harris proposes that these three tales "provide an important conceptual bridge between Lawrence's two drafts of *The Plumed Serpent*" (*Short Fiction of D. H. Lawrence*, 184). I believe that all four of these works depicting female protagonists at the end of their tether comprise for Lawrence another exploratory nexus similar to that involving the miner/miner's wife situation that he wrote out in so many versions (see my discussion of "Odour of Chrysanthemums"). Since these works do explore different possibilities and outcomes, we should not presume that any one of them embodies Lawrence's settled ideas about these issues. Harris seems to agree when she faults Kate Millett for concluding her "scathing analysis" of Lawrence with a discussion of "The Woman Who Rode Away," and failing to mention that he went on to write *St. Mawr* (Harris, *Short Fiction of D. H. Lawrence*, 290).

85. Janice Harris briefly reviews the extensive critical literature on the story, pointing out that "critics tend to praise or disparage the piece on the basis of their evaluation of its mythic dimensions," and noting that "[c]ritics who see problems in the tale question the human implications that lie within or obtrude upon the mythic dimensions" (*Short Fiction of D. H. Lawrence*, 184). But another watershed exists between critics who presume that Lawrence sanctions what the story depicts, and those who do not. Among Lawrence's admirers who see this story negatively is Julian Moynahan, who by his own account has been battling with the story for some years; see his *Deed of Life*, 178, and his "Foreword" to *A Modern Lover and Other Stories* (1969), xvii–xviii.

86. I propose a spectrum among Lawrence's stories in regard to the degree to which they are "about" individual relationships or cultural processes. "Monkey Nuts" and "Tickets, Please" are about individual relationships, but

they reverberate with the context of the postwar situation. "England, My England" is about Egbert and Winifred, but their story embodies a larger story that is going on in England and in Western culture. "The Woman Who Rode Away" is simultaneously about two different levels of process and is as much about the decline of the Indian culture as it is about the woman. "Things" is not so much about the Melvilles as individual persons as it is about the mechanisms by which modernist "idealism" alienates us from vital, changing experience.

87. This view is epitomized by Charles Rossman's essay "Myth and Misunderstanding D. H. Lawrence." Rossman inexplicably presumes that Lawrence wants us to *like* everything about this obviously unpleasant tale. He is critical of myth criticism on the story, saying that it proffers "not the futile destruction of a housewife from Berkeley, but a 'myth of regeneration,' promising renewed vitality for a whole race. Of course, Lawrence *wanted* the tale to be regarded as just such a myth. But to grant Lawrence his own premises in this instance is to accept his rationalization as his true motive, to make wholesome what is really horrible" (82). Later Rossman says, "Lawrence has vented his private animus, projecting it in terms of a religious myth to lend it a specious objectivity and, hence, personal and public acceptability" (97), and subsequently that Lawrence hated the woman and "approves of the Indians' behavior" (99). But it is simpler and less condescending to Lawrence to presume that what shocks and offends us in this story is intended to do so.

88. In the early version of his "The Spirit of Place," Lawrence speaks directly to our need to acknowledge these larger cultural and historic forces: "Also we must wake and sharpen in ourselves the subtle faculty for perceiving the greater inhuman forces that control us. It is our fatal limitation, at the present time, that we can only understand in terms of personal and conscious choice. We cannot see that great motions carry us and bring us to our place before we can even begin to know. We cannot see that invisible winds carry us unwitting, as they carry the locust swarms, and direct us before our knowledge, as they direct the migrating birds" (*The Symbolic Meaning*, 19–20).

89. Janice Harris objects to this last sentence as inconsistent on Lawrence's part, saying that we have seen no such consciousness in the woman (*Short Fiction of D. H. Lawrence*, 185). But the woman is thinking here not of her self, but of the characteristic consciousness of the kind of women among whom she has grown up.

90. In his introduction to *The Dragon of the Apocalypse* Lawrence expresses his fascination with the Chaldean view of the cosmos, saying, "I would like to know the stars again as the Chaldeans knew them, two thousand years before Christ. I would like to be able to put my ego into the sun, and my personality into the moon, and my character into the planets, and live the life of the heavens, as the early Chaldeans did" (*Phoenix*, 298). But Lawrence does not believe such a reorientation easy, or perhaps even possible, for us moderns. A few pages later he says, "We shall not get back the Chaldean vision of

the living heavens" (301), meaning that whatever move we make in that direction will have to be within the context of all that our culture has lived through and experienced since that time—no simple task.

91. In his exploratory fashion, Lawrence in other works of this period depicts other women characters who are at the end of the tether of Western individualism and who are faced with similar prospects and temptations. But Lou Witt in *St. Mawr* and Kate Leslie in *The Plumed Serpent* have more resilience, less romanticism than Mrs. Lederman. Kate is deeply dissatisfied with the vacuity of Western culture and feels the great appeal of the qualitatively different culture that Ramon and Cipriano are trying to resurrect. But she never fully loses sight of the virtual impossibility of transplanting herself into that culture, and she never really relinquishes responsibility for the integrity of her own psyche. And Lou Witt quickly sees through the "primitivism" of Phoenix—another American Indian who has lost faith in the ways of his own people and who defers to the power of the white race. Lawrence describes Phoenix's wish to possess Lou Witt in terms that parallel the motives of these Indians: "It would flatter his vanity and his self-esteem immensely, to possess her. That would be possessing the very clue to the white man's overwhelming world" (*St. Mawr and The Man Who Died* [New York: Vintage Books, 1953], 135).

92. My realization of this truth was clarified by my reading, in George J. Becker, so bald a statement of the opposite view. Speaking of the effects of the tribe's act of sacrificing the woman, Becker says, "Thus the tribe will fulfill prophecy and achieve the power that men must hold for mastery, a power that passes from race to race" (*D. H. Lawrence*, 123). Can anyone really believe that this act of human sacrifice will restore these Indians to their previous rapport with the elements, and restore their belief in themselves as a people? Surely, the act will provide at most a brief sense of power or euphoria, followed by the realization that things have not changed, and consequently that they are worse off than before.

93. In *Fantasia of the Unconscious* Lawrence shows that the inevitable rise and fall of cultures need not leave us utterly without hope: "Floods and fire and convulsions and ice-arrest intervene between the great glamorous civilizations of mankind. But nothing will ever quench humanity and the human potentiality to evolve something magnificent out of a renewed chaos" (*Psychoanalysis and the Unconscious and Fantasia of the Unconscious* [New York: Viking Press, 1960], 56).

The Writer

Introduction

One of the paradoxes revolving around D. H. Lawrence and the short story is that he seems to have thought little specifically about the genre. That Lawrence had virtually nothing to say about the genre is all the more striking because he did write so many literary essays, including several about the novel genre.[1]

In the absence of statements by Lawrence on the short story genre, I have gathered here comments from Lawrence's essays, reviews, miscellaneous published writings, and letters that cast light of various shades on his attitudes regarding the short story. Some of these comments refer to individual writers such as Maupassant, Chekhov, or Verga; others reflect his attitudes toward stories on which he himself was working or those of friends who had asked his advice; still others deal with literary issues such as realism and the idea of authorial effacement. Several of the comments address literary form—a relevant topic since Lawrence's stories have often been described, by his boosters and his detractors alike, as lacking the kind of form regarded as a distinguishing trait of the "modern" short story. Some of the statements printed here are already well known, but most are not. In one sense, all of his essays on the novel are relevant and might have been candidates for reprinting here. But those essays deal specifically with the novel, and they are among Lawrence's best known and most readily available, in *Phoenix* and *Phoenix II*, and more recently in the Cambridge edition of *Study of Thomas Hardy and Other Essays*.

In some of these essays Lawrence singles out the novel, making statements that suggest it to be quite distinct in its capacities and superior to other literary modes. For example, in "Why the Novel Matters," he says, "The Novel is the one bright book of life.... the novel as a tremulation *can* make the whole man-alive tremble. Which is more than poetry, philosophy, science or any other book-tremulation can do," and he also remarks, "To be alive, to be man alive, to be whole man alive: that is the point. And at its best, the novel, and the novel supremely, can help you" (*Study of Thomas Hardy and Other Essays*, 195, 197). In "Morality and the Novel," he says, "The novel is the highest complex of subtle inter-relatedness that man has discovered"; "And of all the art forms, the novel most of all demands the trembling and oscillating of the balance"; and "The novel is a perfect medium for revealing to us the changing rainbow of our living relationships. The novel can help us to live, as nothing else can" (*Study of Thomas Hardy and Other Essays*, 172, 173, 175). I do not think that these statements involve denigration of the short story. Lawrence regarded prose fiction as superior to poetry because it requires writer and reader to engage in a more fully constructed social/cultural world than is necessarily evoked by a poem. The novel is thus marginally superior to the novelette, and to the long short story, and to the short story proper, only because it permits or demands a fuller-scale presentation of such a world. At its best a novel of some 250 to 300 pages simply has the opportunity to call forth a fuller, richer, more variegated world than does a story of some 20 pages. In this alone, I believe, lies the relative superiority of the novel as a form for Lawrence.

The following comments are divided into two sections: Essays, Reviews, and Miscellaneous Published Writings; and Letters. The items in both are arranged chronologically.

Note

1. Dennis Jackson and Fleda Brown Jackson say, "Lawrence himself never made a public statement about the aesthetic of the short story, as he did about the novel, and no doubt partially for that reason, some critics have suggested that he did not really care about the short story form, that he wrote stories just to earn—as he himself put it in a 1912 letter to Edward Garnett—'running money'" (*Critical Essays on D. H. Lawrence* [Boston: G. K. Hall, 1988], 25). But they go on to disagree with this judgment and to cite evidence against it. Ronald P. Draper comments on the lack of statements by Lawrence on the short story and says he seems not to have taken it seriously as a form (*D. H. Lawrence* [New York: Grosset and Dunlap, 1964], 119).

Lawrence's Essays, Reviews, and Miscellaneous Published Writings

Review of Georgian Poetry: 1911–1912

This collection is like a big breath taken when we are waking up after a night of oppressive dreams. The nihilists, the intellectual, hopeless people—Ibsen, Flaubert, Thomas Hardy—represent the dream we are waking from. It was a dream of demolition. Nothing was, but was nothing. Everything was taken from us. And now our lungs are full of air, and our eyes see it is morning, but we have not forgotten the terror of the night. We dreamed we were falling through space into nothingness, and the anguish of it leaves us rather eager.

But we are awake again, our lungs are full of new air, our eyes of morning. The first song is nearly a cry, fear and the remembrance of pain sharpening away the pure music. And that is this book.

The last years have been years of demolition. Because faith and belief were getting pot-bound, and the Temple was made a place to barter sacrifices, therefore faith and belief and the Temple must be broken. This time art fought the battle, rather than science or any new religious faction. And art has been demolishing for us: Nietzsche, the Christian religion as it stood; Hardy, our faith in our own endeavor; Flaubert, our belief in love. Now, for us, it is all smashed, we can see the whole again. We were in prison, peeping at the sky through loop-holes. The great prisoners smashed at the loop-holes, for lying to us. And behold, out of the ruins leaps the whole sky.

*Review of *Georgian Poetry: 1911–1912*, edited by Edward Marsh, first printed in *Rhythm*, March 1913.
**Acknowledgment for right to reprint material from the works and letters of D. H. Lawrence is made to Laurence Pollinger Ltd. and the Estate of Frieda Lawrence Ravagli.

German Books: Thomas Mann

Germany is now undergoing that craving for form in fiction, that passionate desire for the mastery of the medium of narrative, that will of the writer to be greater than and undisputed lord over the stuff he writes, which is figured to the world in Gustave Flaubert.

. . .

. . . [T]his craving for form is the outcome, not of artistic conscience, but of a certain attitude to life. For form is not a personal thing like style. It is impersonal like logic. And just as the school of Alexander Pope was logical in its expressions, so it seems the school of Flaubert is, as it were, logical in its aesthetic form. "Nothing outside the definite line of the book," is a maxim. But can the human mind fix absolutely the definite line of a book, any more than it can fix absolutely any definite line of action for a living being?

. . .

Thomas Mann seems to me the last sick sufferer from the complaint of Flaubert . . . even while he has a rhythm in style, yet his work has none of the rhythm of a living thing, the rise of a poppy, then the after uplift of the bud, the shedding of the calyx and the spreading wide of the petals, the falling of the flower and the pride of the seedhead. There is an unexpectedness in this such as does not come from their carefully plotted developments. Even *Madame Bovary* seems to me dead in respect to the living rhythm of the whole work.

First printed in the *Blue Review*, July 1913.

Study of Thomas Hardy

The adherence to a metaphysic does not necessarily give artistic form. Indeed the overstrong adherence to a metaphysic usually destroys any possibility of artistic form. Artistic form is a revelation of the two principles of Love and Law in a state of conflict and yet reconciled: pure motion struggling against and yet reconciled with the Spirit: active force meeting and overcoming and yet not overcoming inertia. It is the conjunction of the two which makes form. And since the two must always meet under fresh conditions, form must always be different. Each work of art has its own form, which has no relation to any other form.

. . .

It is the novelists and dramatists who have the hardest task in reconciling their metaphysic, their theory of being and knowing, with their living sense of being. Because a novel is a microcosm, and because man in viewing the universe must view it in the light of a theory, therefore every novel must have the background or the structural skeleton of some theory of being, some metaphysic. But the metaphysic must always subserve the artistic purpose beyond the artist's conscious aim. Otherwise the novel becomes a treatise.

And the danger is, that a man shall make himself a metaphysic to excuse or cover his own faults or failure. Indeed, a sense of fault or failure is the usual cause of a man's making himself a metaphysic, to justify himself.

First printed in *Phoenix: The Posthumous Papers of D. H. Lawrence*, edited by Edward D. McDonald. New York: Viking Press, 1936.

Edgar Allan Poe

Poe is rather a scientist than an artist. He is reducing his own self as a scientist reduces a salt in a crucible. It is an almost chemical analysis of the soul and consciousness. Whereas in true art there is always the double rhythm of creating and destroying.

This is why Poe calls his things "tales." They are a concatenation of cause and effect.

His best pieces, however, are not tales. They are more. They are ghastly stories of the human soul in its disruptive throes.

Moreover, they are "love" stories.

Ligeia and *The Fall of the House of Usher* are really love stories.

. . .

In the *Murders in the Rue Morgue* and *The Gold Bug* we have those mechanical tales where the interest lies in the following out of a subtle chain of cause and effect. The interest is scientific rather than artistic, a study in psychologic reactions.

From *Studies in Classic American Literature*, New York: Thomas Seltzer, 1923.

Introduction to *Mastro-don Gesualdo*, by Giovanni Verga

Verga is one of the greatest masters of the short story. In the volume *Novelle Rusticane* and in the volume entitled *Cavalleria Rusticana* are some of the best short stories ever written. They are sometimes as short and as poignant as Chekhov. I prefer them to Chekhov. Yet nobody reads them. They are "too depressing." They don't depress me half as much as Chekhov does. I don't understand the popular taste.

. . .

The trouble with realism—and Verga was a realist—is that the writer, when he is a truly exceptional man like Flaubert or like Verga, tries to read his own sense of tragedy into people much smaller than himself. I think it is a final criticism against *Madame Bovary* that people such as Emma Bovary and her husband Charles simply are too insignificant to carry the full weight of a Gustave Flaubert's sense of tragedy. Emma and Charles Bovary are a couple of little people. Gustave Flaubert is not a little person. But, because he is a realist and does not believe in "heroes," Flaubert insists on pouring his own deep and bitter tragic consciousness into the little skins of the country doctor and his uneasy wife. The result is a discrepancy. *Madame Bovary* is a great book and a very wonderful picture of life. But we cannot help resenting the fact that the great tragic soul of Gustave Flaubert is, so to speak, given only the rather commonplace bodies of Emma and Charles Bovary. There's a misfit. And to get over the misfit, you have to let in all sorts of seams of pity. Seams of pity, which won't be hidden.

. . .

. . . [T]he realistic-democratic age has dodged the dilemma of having no heroes by having every man his own hero. This is reached by what we call subjective intensity, and in this subjectively-intense every-man-his-own-hero business the Russians have carried us to the greatest lengths. The merest scrub of a pick-pocket is so phenomenally aware of his own soul, that we are made to bow down before the

111

imaginary coruscations that go on inside him. That is almost the whole of Russian literature: the phenomenal coruscations of the souls of quite commonplace people.

Of course your soul will coruscate, if you think it does. That's why the Russians are so popular. No matter how much of a shabby animal you may be, you can learn from Dostoievsky and Chekhov, etc., how to have the most tender, unique, coruscating soul on earth. And so you may be most vastly important to yourself. Which is the private aim of all men. The hero had it openly. The commonplace person has it inside himself, though outwardly he says: Of course I'm no better than anybody else! His very asserting it shows he doesn't think it for a second. Every character in Dostoievsky or Chekhov thinks himself *inwardly* a nonesuch, absolutely unique.

First printed in *Phoenix: The Posthumous Papers of D. H. Lawrence*, edited by Edward D. McDonald. New York: Viking Press, 1936.

Preface to *Cavalleria Rusticana,*
by Giovanni Verga

The Chekhovian after-influenza effect of inertia and will-lessness is wearing off, all over Europe. And if Chekhov represents the human being driven into an extremity of self-consciousness and faintly-wriggling inertia, Verga represents him as waking suddenly from inaction to the stroke of revenge. We shall see which of the two visions is more deeply true to life.

"Cavalleria Rusticana" and "La Lupa" have always been hailed as masterpieces of brevity and gems of literary form. Masterpieces they are, but one is now a little sceptical of their form. After the enormous diffusiveness of Victor Hugo, it was perhaps necessary to make the artist more self-critical and self-effacing. But any wholesale creed in art is dangerous. Hugo's romanticism, which consisted in letting himself go, in an orgy of effusive self-conceit, was not much worse than the next creed the French invented for the artist, of self-effacement. Self-effacement is quite as self-conscious, and perhaps even more conceited than letting oneself go. Maupassant's self-effacement becomes more blatant than Hugo's self-effusion. As for the perfection of form achieved—Mérimée achieved the highest, in his dull stories like "Mateo Falcone" and "L'Enlèvement de la Redoute." But they are hopelessly literary, fabricated. So is most of Maupassant. And if *Madame Bovary* has form, it is a pretty flat form.

But Verga was caught up by the grand idea of self-effacement in art. Anything more confused, more silly, really, than the pages prefacing the excellent story "Gramigna's Lover" would be hard to find, from the pen of a great writer. The moment Verga starts talking theories, our interest wilts immediately. The theories were none of his own: just borrowed from the literary smarties of Paris. And poor Verga looks a sad sight in Paris ready-mades. And when he starts putting his theories into practice, and effacing himself, one is far more aware of his

First printed in *Phoenix: The Posthumous Papers of D. H. Lawrence*, edited by Edward D. McDonald. New York: Viking Press, 1936.

interference than when he just goes ahead. Naturally! Because self-effacement is, of course, self-conscious, and any form of emotional self-consciousness hinders a first-rate artist: though it may help the second rate.

Therefore in "Cavalleria Rusticana" and "La Lupa" we are just a bit too much aware of the author and his scissors. He has clipped away too many. The transitions are too abrupt. All is over in a gasp: whereas a story like "La Lupa" covers at least several years of time.

As a matter of fact, we need more looseness. We need an apparent formlessness, definite form is mechanical. We need more easy transition from mood to mood and from deed to deed. A great deal of the meaning of life and of art lies in the apparently dull spaces, the pauses, the unimportant passages. They are truly passages, the places of passing over.

Lawrence's Letters

To Jessie Chambers, [February? 1906]
What am I doing to you? You used to be so vigorous, so full of interest in all sorts of things. Don't take too much notice of me. You mustn't allow yourself to be hurt by Maupassant or by me.

To Blanche Jennings, 13 May 1908
Do you know what I shall do when I am out of college? I shall write drivelling short-stories and the like for money. I am learning quite diligently to play the fool consistently, so that at last I may hire myself out as a jester, a motley to tap folks on the head fairly smartly with a grotesque stick—like Shaw does.

To Louie Burrows, 7 October 1908
The great thing to do in a short story is to select the salient details—a few striking details to make a sudden swift impression. Try to use words vivid and emotion-quickening; give as little explanation as possible . . .; make some parts swifter . . .; avoid bits of romantic sentimentality . . .; select some young fellow of your acquaintance as a type for your lover, and think what he probably would do . . .; be *very careful* of slang; a little is as much as most folks can stand.

To Blanche Jennings, 9 October 1908
Where could I send short stories such as I write? not to any magazine I know of—can you advise me. I will take to writing frivolously and whimsically if I can—if I could but write as I behave!

To Blanche Jennings, 11 November 1908

I consider [Balzac's *Eugénie Grandet*] as perfect a novel as I have ever read. It is wonderfully concentrated; there is nothing superfluous, nothing out of place. The book has that wonderful feeling of inevitableness which is characteristic of the best French novels. It is rather astonishing that we, the cold English, should have to go to the flashy French for level-headed, fair, unrelenting realism. Can you find a grain of sentimentality in *Eugénie*? Can you find a touch of melodrama, or caricature, or flippancy? It is all in tremendous earnestness, more serious than all the profoundities of German thinkers, more affecting than all English bathos. It makes me drop my head and sit silent. Balzac can lay bare the living body of the great Life better than anybody in the world. He doesn't hesitate at the last covering; he doesn't point out the absurdities of the intricate innumerable wrappings and accessories of the body of Life; he goes straight to the flesh; and unlike De Maupassant or Zola, he doesn't inevitably light on a wound, or a festering sore. Balzac is magnificent and supreme; he is not mysterious nor picturesque, so one never sees his portrait.

To Blanche Jennings, 15 December 1908

Referring to Balzac. Do sometime, get a few more vols of him from Everyman. Begin with *Old Goriot*—then try the *Asses Skin*—then *Atheists Mass*. But I remember that the Walter Scott people publish a fine collection of Balzac's short stories for 1/–. You must not fall out with the homilies of so old a writer as Balzac. Think of what one is treated to in Scott and Thackeray—and George Eliot by way of padding and moral and reflection, and you'll see that Balzac lets you off cheap.

To Louie Burrows, advising her about a short story she is writing, 23 January 1910

"The Chimney Sweeper" is much improved. I think' [*sic*] You need, I think, to elaborate a bit: do a bit of character drawing, and give your locality: you want to give more setting: the figures are all right, but examine the scene *"pictorially"*—it is not there. Gather the picture—get the essentials for *description*—present to the eye. The conversation is very amusing. I should offer it to the *Guardian*. You have a certain quaint talent of your own, but it is superficial. Accept it as such—and make the best of it—then you'll do things very likely as good as W. W. Jacobs. . . .

You must study the presentation—be a little more accurate—for instance, would they see the white and blue of the eyes of a man lifted up against the sky, therefore in shadow?—would the creeper in the chimney see "white flesh"? Why did the kid do it? Where is the place? Describe the seen [*sic*] "particularly," and the butcher, and Siah—put a paragraph or two in front to show *why* the sweep should behave so— don't tell us, show him in the situation which leads up to it. Then send the tale to the *Strand*—they would very probably have it.

Mrs. Jones likes the tale very much. Get W W Jacobs out of the sevenpenny Nelsons, and read his amusing tales, and study their development. You should do as well. [The only Jacobs book available in that series at this time was *The Lady of the Barge.* Valerie Shaw points out the similarity between this advice and that given by Chekov to his brother in a letter of May 10, 1886; see Shaw, *The Short Story: A Critical Introduction*, 152.]

To Louie Burrows, 17 December 1910

"Garçon, un bock!—that's a very ugly tale of Maupassant[']s. (*Letters*, I: 206)

To Louie Burrows, 22 December 1910

And all I can give you is this volume of Gorki: which I spotted for you on Saturday, and which is a fine volume, but don't let your father read it: put it in your bottom drawer. Poor Gorki: I'm very much an English equivalent of his. I have not read all the tales, so I'll have a look at them when I'm over. (*Letters*, I: 209; the volume was perhaps R. Nisbet Bain's translation, *Tales from Gorki*)

To Louie Burrows, 12 April 1911

I've finished the fourth story—its the "White Stocking" written up. Mac says it is fantastic. Really, its not up to a great deal. But I intended to do four, and four are done.

To Martin Secker, 12 June 1911

There have appeared in print, in the *English Review*, two and two only of my tales. Because nobody wanted the things, I have not troubled to write any. So that, at present, I have two good stories published, three very decent ones lying in the hands of the Editor of the *English Review*, another good one at home, and several slight things sketched out and neglected.

To Edward Garnett, 10 January 1912

Harrison sent me back this story ["The White Stocking"] yesterday, and he's publishing one I don't like a bit—a poor one. ["Second Best," published in the *English Review*, February 1912, 461–69] ... P.S. The books have just come. I love books of Short stories. Andreyev is not so burningly interesting, is he?

To Edward Garnett, 21 January 1912
I like the first two stories of Gertrude Bone immensely—she is wonderfully perceptive there. She's got a lot of poetic feeling, a lot of perceptivity, but she seems scarcely able to concentrate it on her people she is studying: at least not always. Something in Andreyev makes him rather uninteresting to me, and [Gissing's] *House of Cobwebs* is, as Seccombe suggests, chiefly of interest as footnotes on Gissing. Gissing hasn't enough energy, enough consanguinity, to capture me. But I esteem him a great deal. [The Bone reference is probably to *Provincial Tales* (Duckworth, 1904), so that the first two stories would be "Poverty" and "The Right Eye." The Gissing reference is to Thomas Seccombe's "The Work of George Gissing: an Introductory Survey," prefixed to Gissing's *House of Cobwebs* (1906) xlviii-xlix.]

To Walter de la Mare, 1 March 1912
The Return is one of the books that lives with me.

To Edward Garnett, 4 August 1912
I had a letter from Harrison re a story. His is a wishy-washy noodle, God help me. My stories are too "steaming" for him. . . . I am going to write six short stories. I must try and make running money.

To Arthur McLeod, 4 October 1912
I have read *Anna of the Five Towns* today, because it is stormy weather. . . . I hate Bennett's resignation. Tragedy ought really to be a great kick at misery. But *Anna of the Five Towns* seem like an acceptance—so does all the modern stuff since Flaubert. I hate it. I want to wash again quick, wash off England, the oldness and grubbiness and despair. (*Letters*, I: 459)

To Edward Garnett, 30 October–2 November 1912
Thanks so much for the books. I hate Strindberg—he seems unnatural, forced, a bit indecent—a bit wooden, like Ibsen, a bit skinerupty. The Conrad, after months of Europe, makes me furious—and the stories are *so* good. But why this giving in before you start that pervades all Conrad and such folks—the Writers among the Ruins. I can't forgive Conrad for being so sad and for giving in.

To Edward Garnett, 19 November 1912 (at the end of a letter from Lawrence to Garnett defending the form of the rewritten *Sons and Lovers*, Frieda von Richthofen Weekley adds a postscript that is relevant, since it conveys ideas they must have been debating): I also feel as if I ought to say something about L.s formlessness. I don't think he has "no form": I used to. But now I think that anybody must see in Paul

Morel [in *Sons and Lovers*] the hang of it. . . . I think the honesty, the vividness of a book suffers if you subject it to "form." I have heard so much about "form" with Ernst, why are you English so keen on it, their own form wants smashing in almost any direction, but they cant come out of their snail house. I know it is so much safer. That's what I love Lawrence for, that he is so plucky and honest in his work, he dares to come out in the open and plants his stuff down bald and naked, really he is the only revolutionary worthy of the name, that I know, any new thing must find a new shape, then afterwards one can call it "art." I hate art, it seems like grammar, wants to make a language all grammar, language was first and then they abstracted a grammar; I quite firmly believe that L is quite great in spite of his "gaps." Look at the vividness of his stuff, it knocks you down I think. It is perhaps too "intimate" comes too close, but I believe that is youth and he has not done, not by long chalks. . . . We *all* go for things, look at them with preconceived notions, things must have a "precedence." We have lost the faculty of seeing things unprejudiced, live off our own bat, think off our own free mind.

To Ernest Collings, 24 December 1912

I always say, my motto is "Art for my sake." If I *want* to write, I write—and if I don't want to, I won't. The difficulty is to find exactly the form one's passion—work is produced by passion with me, like kisses—is it with you?—wants to take.

I am glad you prefer "Odour of Chrysanthemums"—I do. But the literary people who have talked to me, so many of them, prefer "Stained Glass." But I hate the conventionalized literary person—of the type I call "Asphodels." . . . They want me to have form: that means, they want me to have their pernicious ossiferous skin-and-grief form, and I won't.

To Arthur McLeod, 23 April 1913

I am wading through [H. G. Wells's] *New Machiavelli*. It depresses me. I sometimes find it too long. But it is awfully interesting. I like Wells, he is so warm, such a passionate declaimer or reasoner or whatever you like. But ugh—he hurts me. He always seems to be looking at life as a cold and hungry little boy in the street stares at a shop where there is hot pork. I do like him and esteem him, and wish I knew half as much about things. . . .

Pray to your gods for me that *Sons and Lovers* shall succeed. People should begin to take me seriously now. And I do so break my heart over England, when I read the *New Machiavelli*. And I am so sure that only through a readjustment between men and women, and a making free and healthy of the sex, will she [England] get out of her present atrophy. Oh Lord, and if I don't "subdue my art to a metaphysic," as somebody very beautifully said of Hardy, I do write because I want folk—English folk—to alter, and have more sense.

To Arthur McLeod, 2 June 1914

I have been interested in the futurists. I got a book of their poetry—a very fat book too—and [a] book of pictures—and I read Marinetti's and Paolo Buzzi's manifestations and essays—and Sofficis essays on cubism and futurism. It interests me very much. I like it because it is the applying to emotions of the purging of the old forms and senti-mentalities. I like it for its saying—enough of this sickly cant, let us be honest and stick by what is in us. Only when folk say, "let us be honest and stick by what is in us"—they always mean, stick by those things that have been thought horrid, and by those alone. They want to deny every scrap of tradition and experience, which is silly. They are very young, infantile, college-student and medical-student at his most bla-tant. But I like them. Only I don't believe in them. I agree with them about the weary sickness of pedantry and tradition and inertness, but I don't agree with them as to the cure and the escape. They will progress down the purely male or intellectual or scientific line. They will even use their intuition for intellectual or scientific purpose. The one thing about their art is that it *isn't* art, but ultra scientific attempts to make diagrams of certain psychic or mental states. It is ultra-ultra intellectual, going beyond Maeterlinck and the Symbolistes, who are intellectual. There isn't one trace of naïveté in the works—though there's plenty of naïveté in the authors. It's the most self-conscious, intentional, pseudo scientific stuff on the face of the earth. . . .

I think the only re-sourcing of art, re-vivifying it, is to make it more the joint work of man and woman. I think *the* one thing to do, is for men to have courage to draw nearer to women, expose themselves to them, and be altered by them: and for women to accept and admit men. That is the only way for art and civilization to get a new life, a new start—by bringing themselves together, men and women—re-vealing themselves each to the other, gaining great blind knowledge and suffering and joy, which it will take a big further lapse of civiliza-tion to exploit and work out. Because the source of all life and knowl-edge is in man and woman, and the source of all living is in the interchange and the meeting and mingling of these two: man-life and woman-life, man-knowledge and women-knowledge, man-being and woman-being.

To Edward Garnett, 5 June 1914 (writing about the novel he was composing, which became *The Rainbow*)
I think the book is a bit futuristic—quite unconsciously so. But when I read Marinetti—"the profound intuitions of life added one to the other, word by word, according to their illogical conception, will give us the general lines of an intuitive physiology of matter" I see something of what I am after. I translate him clumsily, and his Italian is obfuscated—and I don't care about physiology of matter—but somehow—that which is physic—non-human, in humanity, is more interesting to me than the old-fashioned human element—which causes one to conceive a character in a certain moral scheme and make him consistent. The certain moral scheme is what I object to. In Turguenev, and in Tolstoi, and in Dostoievski, the moral scheme into which all the characters fit—and it is nearly the same scheme—is, whatever the extraordinariness of the characters themselves, dull, old, dead. When Marinetti writes: "it is the solidity of a blade of steel that is interesting by itself, that is, the incomprehending and inhuman alliance of its molecules in resistance to, let us say, a bullet. The heat of a piece of wood or iron is in fact more passionate, for us, than the laughter or tears of a woman—then I know what he means. He is stupid, as an artist, for contrasting the heat of the iron with the laugh of the woman. Because what is interesting in the laugh of the woman is the same as the binding of the molecules of steel or their action in heat: it is the inhuman will, call it physiology, or like Marinetti—physiology of matter, that fascinates me. I don't care so much about what the woman *feels*—in the ordinary usage of the word. That presumes an ego to feel with. I only care about what the woman *is*—what she *is*—inhumanly, physiologically, materially—according to the use of the word: but for me, what she is as a phenomenon (or representing some greater inhuman will), instead of what she feels according to the human conception. That is where the futurists are stupid. Instead of looking for the new human phenomenon, they will look only for the phenomena of the science of physics to be found in the human being. They are crassly stupid. But if anyone would give them eyes, they would pull the right apples off the tree, for their stomachs are true in appetite. You mustn't look in my novel for the old stable ego of the character. There is another ego, according to whose action the individual is unrecognizable, and passes through, as it were, allotropic states which it needs a deeper sense than any we've been used to exercise,

120

to discover are states of the same single radically-unchanged element. (Like as diamond and coal are the same pure single element of carbon. the ordinary novel would trace the history of the diamond—but I say "diamond, what! This is carbon." And my diamond might be coal or soot, and my theme is carbon.)

You must not say my novel is shaky—It is not perfect, because I am not expert in what I want to do. But it is the real thing, say what you like. And I shall get my reception, if not now, then before long. Again I say, don't look for the development of the novel to follow the lines of certain characters: the characters fall into the form of some other rhythmic form, like when one draws a fiddle-bow across a fine tray delicately sanded, the sand takes lines unknown.

To J. B. Pinker, 16 December 1915

Tell Arnold Bennett that all rules of construction hold good only for novels which are copies of other novels. A book which is not a copy of other books has its own construction, and what he calls faults, he being an old imitator, I call characteristics.

To Carlo Linati, 22 January 1925

But really, Signor Linati, do you think that books should be sort of toys, nicely built up of observations or sensations, all finished and complete?—I don't. To me, even Synge, whom I admire very much indeed, is a bit too rounded off and, as it were, put on the shelf to be looked at. I can't bear art that you can walk round and admire. A book should be either a bandit or a rebel or a man in a crowd. People should either run for their lives, or come under the colours, or say *how do you do?* I hate the actor and audience business. An author should be in among the crowd, kicking their shins or cheering them on to some mischief or merriment—That rather cheap seat in the gods where one sits with fellows like Anatole France and benignly looks down on the foibles, follies, and frenzies of so-called fellow-men, just annoys me. After all, the world is *not* a stage—not to me: nor a theatre: nor a show-house of any sort. And art, especially novels, are not little theatres where the reader sits aloft and watches—like a god with a twenty-Lira ticket—and sighs, commiserates, condones and smiles.—That's what you want a book to be: because it leaves you so safe and so superior, with your two-dollar ticket to the show. And that's what my books are not and never will be. You need not complain that I don't subject the intensity of my vision—or whatever it is—to some vast and imposing rhythm—by which you mean isolate it on to a stage so that you can look down on it like a god who has a ticket to the show. I never will: and you will never have that satisfaction from me. Stick to Synge, Anatole France, Sophocles: they will never kick the footlights even. But whoever reads me will be in the thick of the scrimmage, and if he doesn't like it—if he wants a safe seat in the audience—let him read somebody else.

From *The Letters of D. H. Lawrence*. Cambridge: Cambridge University Press, 1979–.

PART 3

The Critics

Introduction

This section reprints excerpts from discussions dealing with Lawrence's distinctive use of the genre, with the various types or modes of short story he wrote, with the phases his work in the genre went through, or with his forebears or descendants in the genre. I have preserved the continuity of these discussions, but have deleted summaries of or lengthy quotations from the stories, as well as explications of individual stories, except where these explications pointedly illustrate some more general thesis.

Lawrence's relationship to the short story genre remains in several respects an enigma: in terms of his attitude toward the genre, in terms of the question of influences exerted on him by earlier short story writers or the influence he exerted on later story writers, in terms of categorizing his stories as "realistic" or "fabulistic," in terms even of trying, often without much success, to articulate what is distinctive about his best stories.

Some general discussions categorize the stories into various types, or specify various phases into which the stories fall. But there is little consensus among critics as to which stories fall into which categories. While Lawrence's stories undoubtedly do change over time, the viability, the feasibility, of designating "phases" of his work is vitiated by several factors. For one, Lawrence's practice of revising his stories for every new publication makes it difficult to keep the phases distinct; he did often rework his stories so drastically that the first version of a story and the version eventually published in book form can be separated by considerable evolution in his ideas and techniques.

On the other hand, designating phases in his stories is made harder by the ubiquity throughout Lawrence's career of his capacity for deft, economical presentation of the dramatic situation and of crucial aspects of his characters; of striking insight into his characters' motivations, both profound and superficial; and of his capacity to suggest or display the complexity of these motives. Even Lawrence's earliest stories are never simply realistic, in the vein of Maupassant, and even his mythic or fabulistic stories often involve so much psychological analysis and insight that the reader must maintain a significant degree of psychological vigilance to appreciate these qualities. To a great extent, general discussion of Lawrence's short stories consists either of sheer encomium or vague generalizations, or of doubtful groupings or categorizations of the stories, and the generally bland nature of these discussions testifies to the difficulty of categorizing or labeling Lawrence's short stories.

Another topic often dealt with in the general discussions is the relationships between the stories and the novels. One generalization that emerged early on and has since been frequently repeated is that, because of the constraints inherent in the genre, the quality of Lawrence's art in the short story is generally higher than in his novels. But such claims reflect an unwillingness to grant Lawrence's novels their distinctive modes of exploration and presentation, and they seem as well to involve an implicit denigration of the short story genre by suggesting that the genre per se protects Lawrence from failure— as if there were not as many opportunities for failure in the short story as in the novel. Another related idea is that Lawrence's real achievement, the real progress of his soul, can be traced in the novels more readily than in the stories.

More problematic is the question of whether Lawrence breaks new ground in the stories, or whether he simply clears and domesticates terrain first explored in the novels: are the stories to any degree the growing tip of Lawrence's oeuvre, or (as several critics have claimed) merely the easy consolidation of gains made through novels? Once again, this seems a specious issue, arising out of a failure to acknowledge the significantly different scale, and thus potentiality, of the two genres, and failure as well to recognize the complex symbiosis among Lawrence's works of any given period, including his more philosophical essays, such that no one genre is the sole field of his development.

Surely, studies that examine the rewriting Lawrence did for the stories in the *Prussian Officer* volume show that qualitative improvements were made in the stories from draft to draft, improvements especially in the presentation of the implicit, unarticulated aspects of the characters' psyches, and in the ways the "individual" psyche shades off into both the cultural psyche and the circumambient natural scene. These were exactly the kinds of development going on in the successive rewritings of *Sons and Lovers* and then of *The Sisters*. Finally, then, most of these judgments about the relative artistic quality and exploratory nature of Lawrence's stories and novels arise from different scales of possibility and exploration provided by these two genres.

Another striking feature of criticism of Lawrence's stories is the great variability in evaluation of individual stories even among critics who respect Lawrence and see him as a first-rate writer of stories. This low or even harshly negative evaluation by one critic of a work extolled by another arises from several factors. One mundane factor that must be acknowledged is simply the flagging of critical attentiveness and empathy that often comes into play in reading Lawrence because of the great demands, intellectual, aesthetic, and moral, he places on his readers. Readers feel some strain of this sort if they read too long in some of his novels, and it comes into play as well in reading a number of his shorter works in succession. Quite simply, it is hard to maintain the attentive engagement and the moral and aesthetic responsiveness Lawrence's works require.

Another source of critical variability, especially in regard to works that deal with unpleasant events, such as "The Princess" or "The Woman Who Rode Away" or "None of That," is the critic's unwillingness to recognize that Lawrence often dramatizes and explores unappealing features of our individual or cultural life, and that by no means does he sanction the events within such stories. While Lawrence may sympathize with several of the characters in such stories, there may not be any character whose actions he sanctions. Undoubtedly readers are presented with a challenge when Lawrence empathizes with characters whose actions he deplores, such as Egbert in "England, My England," or the woman or the Indians in "The Woman Who Rode Away." This kind of critical misperception comes into play especially in regard to the stories that explore masculine attempts at dominance (the assumption being that Lawrence wishes the would-be dominator to win out, which cannot be taken for granted), or that explore the individual and cultural drift toward death Lawrence felt was so pervasive a tendency in our culture.

In this collection, I reprint only a small number of the general statements about Lawrence's short stories. Not all of the important statements about Lawrence's short stories lend themselves to excerpting. I have conformed punctuation to American conventions, and have included all footnotes, often expanded to provide full publication information, or—in the case of letters—updated to the Cambridge edition.

H. E. Bates

[Lawrence's] stories are always an expression of a more direct, more controlled, and more objective art. In them Lawrence has no time to preach, to lose his temper, to go mystical, or to persuade the reader to listen to him by the doubtful process of shouting at the top of his voice and finally kicking him downstairs. Lawrence is for once bound to say what he has to say within reasonable, even strict, limits of time and space. Ordinarily dictatorial, Lawrence is here dictated to by the form he has chosen. The results have little of the slobbering hysteria of the later novels; they are again and again a superb expression of Lawrence's greatest natural gifts, sensibility, vision, a supreme sense of the physical (whether beautiful or ugly, human or otherwise), an uncanny sense of place, and a flaming vitality. Unobscured by hysteria, by the passion of theoretical gospels, these qualities shine through three-quarters of the forty stories that Lawrence wrote.

. . .

Clearly form was not Lawrence's primary contribution to the short story; nor, as with Katherine Mansfield, oblique narration; nor, as with Hemingway, a revaluation of style. Like Sherwood Anderson (with whom it is significant that he has often been compared) Lawrence turned his back on the conventionalized story in which most things hinged on artificially created problems or situations, and set to work to interpret his own people and the background of pit-heads, working-class houses, bluebell woods and hills, against which they lived. That, to Lawrence, must have seemed a very natural thing to do. Yet because Lawrence saw people as people his work was constantly stigmatized as shocking by the generation which had eagerly accepted the false and sadistic imperialism of Kipling and the scientific romanticism of Wells. Yet Lawrence, being true to his own vision, will always be closer to life than either Kipling or Wells, and in that respect alone

From *The Modern Short Story: A Critical Survey*. London: Michael Joseph, 1972. (First published in 1941.) Chapter IX is "Lawrence and the Writers of Today," 194–213. Reprinted by permission of the Estate of H. E. Bates.

he set an example, as Anderson did in America, which a new decade of writers eagerly followed. Among the young short-story writers of 1940, you will find none, I think, who owe any important debt to Kipling or Wells; but you will find many who, as they depict the immediate life about them, have Lawrence to thank for the example.

Eudora Welty

In stories today, form, however acutely and definitely it may be felt, does not necessarily imply a formal structure. It is not accounted for by structure, rather. A story with a "pattern," an exact kind of design, may lack a more compelling over-all quality which we call form. Edgar Allan Poe and other writers whose ultimate aim depended on pattern, on a perfect and dovetailing structure (note the relation to puzzles and detection and mystery here), might have felt real horror at a story by D. H. Lawrence first of all because of the unmitigated shapelessness of Lawrence's narrative. Lawrence's world of action and conversation is as far from the frozen perfection, the marblelike situations, of Poe as we can imagine; Lawrence's story world is a shambles—a world just let go, like a sketchy housekeeper's un-straightened-up room. More things are important than this dust! Lawrence would say, and he would be as right as the crier of that cry always is.

And what about his characters? Are they real, recognizable, neat men and women? Would you know them if you saw them? Not even, I think, if they began to speak on the street as they speak in the stories, in the very same words—they would only appear as deranged people. For the truth seems to be that Lawrence's characters don't really speak their words—not conversationally, not to one another; they are *not* speaking on the street, but are playing like fountains or radiating like the moon or storming like the sea, or their silence is the silence of wicked rocks. It is borne home to us that Lawrence is writing of our human relationships on earth in terms of eternity, and these terms set Lawrence's form.

The author himself appears in authorship in phases like the moon, and sometimes blesses us and sometimes smites us while we stand there under him. But we see that his plots and his characters are alike sacrificed to something; there is something which Lawrence considers

From "The Reading and Writing of Short Stories," *Atlantic Monthly*, March 1949, 47–48. Copyright © 1949 by Eudora Welty: © copyright renewed 1977 by Eudora Welty. Reprinted by permission of Russell and Volkening as agents for the author.

as transcending them both. Others besides him have thought that something does. But Lawrence alone, that I have knowledge of now, thinks the transcending thing is found direct through the sense. It is the world of the senses that Lawrence writes in, works in, thinks in, takes as his medium—and if that is strange to us, isn't the loss ours? Through this world he will send his story. It is the plot too; it is his story's reason for being, with sex the channel the senses most deeply, mysteriously, run through, cutting down through layers and centuries and country after country of hypocrisy. . . .

D. H. Lawrence is somewhat like the True Princess, who felt beneath forty mattresses that there was a pea under her. Lawrence is as sensitive to falsity as the True Princess was to the pea. And he is just as sure to proclaim the injury.

How can he be so quarrelsome with us while at the same time he is enrapturing us with his extraordinary powers to make us see and feel beauty? But my feeling toward his writing is my feeling towards greatness anywhere. Take it—take it all. It is no laughing matter. It is more pertinent to give in to that beauty of his and better to grit our teeth at his cruelty—for he is cruel—than to laugh at or be annoyed by the shambles he makes of the everyday world.

We all use the everyday world in our stories, and some of us feel inclined or even bound to give it at least a cursory glance and treatment, but Lawrence does not care. He feels no responsibility there at all. He does not care if the mechanics and props of everyday life suffer in his stories from distortion unto absurdity, if his narrative thins and frays away into silliness. Those things aren't what he's concerned with. His plots might remind you of some kind of tropical birds—that are awkward in structure and really impossible-looking when they're on the ground, and then when they take wing and fly, a miracle happens. All that clumsiness and outrageousness is gone; the bird's body becomes astonishingly functional, and iridescent in flight.

Graham Hough

So far, by confining ourselves to Lawrence's major novels we have been able to trace a fairly continuous and consistent course of development. This continuity is found in the major fiction alone. If we take as our text the shorter stories and tales, and study them chronologically as we did the novels, the sense of reading a series, of watching the gradual unfolding of a personality is absent. By themselves the stories present no consistent pattern; though they are full of illuminating parallels and cross-references to the novels, the links among the tales themselves are fewer. And the tales themselves include a wide diversity of types. They vary in length, for instance, from the merest sketches or anecdotes, such as "Smile" or "Things," to what are in effect short novels, with full development and a wide range of character and incident, like "St. Mawr" or "The Captain's Doll." And in between is the normal long-short story which Lawrence utilises with success at all stages of his career. It does not look as if he ever gave much conscious thought to these varying scales on which fiction can be practised.... The range and comprehensiveness of the plots, and the length at which they are treated seems, in fact, to be mainly decided by the amount of time, material, and energy Lawrence has to spare from his longer fictions. The importance he attached to the stories and the degree of achievement is equally variable.... "The Woman Who Rode Away" is in an obvious sense the by-product of *The Plumed Serpent;* yet it is far superior in aesthetic organisation. Such stories as "Smile" or "Rawdon's Roof" are trivial or ill-tempered *jeux d'esprit;* while "The Woman Who Rode Away" and "The Man Who Died" are the vehicles of Lawrence's deepest intuitions. The two last are also sharply distinguished from all the others by making little attempt at realism. In them we are approaching the realm of myth and

From *The Dark Sun: A Study of D. H. Lawrence* (London: Duckworth, 1956), Chapter 3, "The Tales," pp. 167–90, passim. Reprinted with the permission of Macmillan Publishing Company. Copyright © 1957 by Graham Goulder Hough.

fable; in "The Fox" and "Odour of Chrysanthemums" we are firmly planted on common earth.

With all this diversity there is perhaps only one thing the tales have in common—and that is something negative; they are *not* the growing points of Lawrence's fiction. Perhaps this is in the end the only way of distinguishing between what are conventionally called his short stories and what are conventionally called his novels. It is never, I think, in the short stories that a new phase of Lawrence's development opens. His new ideas are hammered out in the long novels (that is why a consistent development can be seen through them); and the short stories are related to these arduous voyages of exploration in a variety of ways. Sometimes they are simply surplus material—as many of the early stories seem to be left over from *The White Peacock* and *Sons and Lovers*. Sometimes they are more compact and fully realised versions of what a novel was trying to do, like "The Woman Who Rode Away." Sometimes they are quite independent creations, in the mode of whatever long novel he was engaged on at the time. Precisely because it is not in these shorter tales that the original exploration is done, they are often superior in artistic organisation to the long exploratory novels. In a restricted form, preaching and repetition are bound to be kept to a minimum; and those who say, as many do, that Lawrence's best work is in his shorter pieces have much reason on their side. In sustained realisation, in formal completeness there is certainly nothing to better the best of his shorter tales. But simply to prefer them probably implies some reduction in the importance of Lawrence as a whole; by the student of Lawrence the stories can best be seen in relation to the solid range of his longer works. . . .

The early stories are very unequal in sheer technical competence. "A Fragment of Stained Glass" is a feeble juvenility, with its laborious but pointless indirect narration and its absurd attempt at historical evocation. There are two stories directly concerned with the Miriam relationship: "A Modern Lover" and, rather more developed, "The Shades of Spring." . . . The constant re-handling of this theme reveals an unsolved personal problem, and neither story makes any advance towards a solution. This sounds irrelevant, but it is not quite; the integrity of Lawrence's writing on this theme depends on progress in self-knowledge. Here we have a mere compulsive circling round. Both stories are nearer to *The White Peacock* than to *Sons and Lovers*, and the uneasy element of half-deprecatory preening in the presentation of the hero is even more apparent. "Second Best" presents a similar situation from the girl's point of view, and is the better for the hero's absence.

A far stronger group of tales is the one that takes up the firm objective manner of the early part of *Sons and Lovers,* and fixes itself upon the portrayal of working-class life in a mining district. "The White Stocking" and "Odour of Chrysanthemums" are the best of these. Both are admirable. They show little trace of the characteristic Laurentian promise, but they are complete achievements. In them, as in all the less intimately personal parts of *Sons and Lovers,* we see what Lawrence might easily have become (what in passing, perhaps, he did become)—the classic novelist of the English workers. "The White Stocking" . . . is absolutely uncontrived, in detail authentic at every point, and formally complete. "Odour of Chrysanthemums" is on the tragically familiar theme of the miner brought home dead after a pit accident. He has been a drinker and a bad husband, and it is from this ironic standpoint that the tragedy is seen. Depth and complexity are added in the final scene by showing it through the eyes of two women, his wife and his mother, with radically different attitudes. If we do not require Lawrence's peculiar kind of insight, with all its possibilities and all its perils, these stories are as perfect achievements, on their own scale, as anything he wrote.

"Daughters of the Vicar" is a more ambitious tale, in length, elaborateness of pattern and social range. It broaches some of the familiar Laurentian themes—the emotional etiolation of the well-bred, the lady who allies herself with a man of the people. And they appear in this story without tendentiousness, as natural outcome of the social circumstances. . . . The elder sister and her husband owe something to Dorothea and Casaubon in *Middlemarch,* and the patient objectivity of the treatment shows, I think, the influence of George Eliot in general. This story also marks the beginning of Lawrence's criticism of English class-relations: though without the verve of some of his later efforts in the same direction, it is remarkable for its moderation and for the refusal of the picture to step outside the frame.

Two stories in this period are of quite a different kind—"The Prussian Officer" and "The Thorn in the Flesh." They are both studies of German militarism and its impact on simple lives; and the outside stimulus to them can only have been provided by a brief contact with German military authorities in the few weeks after Lawrence first left England. They mark a decisive step in the development of his literary imagination. Up to now he has always written of a world that was familiar to him and on themes very close to his own experience. Here he is making a leap into a world of which he can only have had the merest glimpse; yet there is not the slightest failure of imaginative realisation. "The Prussian Officer" is a repulsively powerful story of a sadistic, quasi-homosexual relation between the officer and his peasant orderly. The focus is on the psychology of the individuals, but the implied picture of the society in which all this could occur is equally compelling. Nothing of the sort had ever been part of Lawrence's experience, and this is perhaps the place to remark on a prevailing characteristic of the short stories. Whatever depth of personal experience lies behind them, they are far more objective and self-contained than the long novels. The novels constantly spill over into Lawrence's personal life, and can hardly be explained without reference to it. The outerworld is used as the vehicle of an expanded metaphor for a process going on in the depths of his own psyche. The short stories, with two notable exceptions, are more the result, that is to say, of observation, intuitively deepened and expanded, but still observation of an outward reality, ending in a creation that has been completely externalised, completely separated from the creator. And that, no doubt, the critic is bound to add, is just what artistic creations ought to be. A result of this is a quickening of the normal novelist's gifts and a revelation of how many of them Lawrence possessed. They are revealed abundantly, to be sure, in the novels; but there they tend to be overlaid by other less usual ones. Lawrence professed himself uninterested in character in the conventional sense; and it is true that many of his major personages live in our minds chiefly as depersonalized representatives of certain states of mind. Incident and circumstance are present less for their own sake than for their part in revealing some train of development quite independent of them. In the short stories character of the self-subsistent, recognizable kind comes into its own again. There are very few of these disguised representations of Lawrence himself that we have learnt to recognize in the novels. The Prussian captain, Banford and March, Countess Hannele and Mrs. Witt assume the status of people that we know, as Miriam, Birkin, Lilly and Don Ramon hardly do. And since the short story must inevitably have a discernible incidental focus of some kind, we see them more completely involved in action.

The next group of stories, the *England, My England* volume, illustrates these points well enough. They are competent, undoctrinaire and spring more from a response to the outer world than from any inner necessity. The title-story was almost a transcript from life, and even Lawrence felt himself to blame for employing an actual situation so crudely. Its motive is the critical response to English society that is found also in *The Rainbow* and *Women in Love*. In the early Midland novels Lawrence had portrayed, analysed but hardly criticised the society around him. After all, he had never known anything else; for him it was the normal world. Travel and widening social horizons were to change all this. Extended contact with the intelligentsia, the educated middle and upper class (Lawrence probably had more of it at this period than at any other) made him increasingly aware of his own difference from them, of the different scale of values in which he had been brought up. The note of rather strident class-awareness, soon to become familiar throughout his work, makes its first appearance in "England, My England."

. . .

The rest of the stories in the volume are a mixed bag. They show Lawrence's powers working freely and with ease, but none are in the first rank. "Monkey Nuts" and "Tickets, Please" do not attempt any great seriousness; and "The Primrose Path" and "Fannie [sic] and Annie" come to less than they promise at first. The most considerable are "You Touched Me," "Samson and Delilah" and "The Horse-Dealer's Daughter." All are on English themes; for some of them Lawrence returns to the Midlands, but not at all in the old spirit. There is no trace of autobiography, and the new interests of *Women in Love* have succeeded those of *Sons and Lovers*. Relations between men and women are always relations of conflict, and lovers rarely seem ever to have any ordinary human understanding of each other; all the stress is on bonds other than the conscious ones. In "Samson and Delilah" a man comes back to claim the wife he deserted fifteen years before. He has a very tough reception and is violently thrown out. But he comes again, and in the end is tacitly accepted. There is a pull between the two of them stronger than the conscious emotions of either.... The situations described [in "Horse-Dealer's Daughter" and "You Touched Me"] would not themselves seem odd or out of place in any ordinary short story. Their peculiarity in Lawrence is that in every case a claim, a bond or an attractive force exerts itself in flat opposition to the normal sentimental disposition of the characters. Of course it is no new thing in fiction for the odious man whom the heroine cannot abide in the first chapter to become the accepted lover in the last. But then the

greatest pains are taken to make the overt sentimental sequence cor-
respond to the operation of the unconscious forces. Any experienced
novel-reader can see at the start that Elizabeth Bennet is going to
marry Darcy; but the latter part of the book is largely occupied in ex-
plaining the process that makes it psychologically possible for her to
do so. No such explanations can be given in these stories of
Lawrence—or, indeed, in most of the personal relations in his works.
It is this in part that gives them their disconcerting air of harshness
and cruelty. People are always being driven to do just what they do
not want to do—women marry the men they hate without apparently
modifying their hatred; men marry women who are certain to make
them unhappy. Lawrence feels the primacy of unconsciousness and
unrecognised forces so strongly that he must show them harshly victo-
rious over all opposition. A harmonious accommodation between conscious and unconscious would not serve his end, however frequently
this occurs in normal experience. It is often said in consequence that
he fails to portray normal experience, and there is something in it. In
life, after all, there are calms between the storms, and Lawrence is apt
to pass over them in a paragraph; he is little interested in the flavour of
ordinary daily intercourse. Yet the violent oppositions, the abrupt
changes of front that abound in his stories, are rarely hard to credit;
they are probably more disconcerting to the amateur of conventional
fiction than they are to the observer of life as it is lived.

. . .

[The complete Lawrence that we know] returns in a more familiar
guise in the Mexican stories. There are three of them—"The
Princess," "The Woman Who Rode Away" and "St. Mawr"—all
longish tales and all belonging to the *Plumed Serpent* period. "The
Woman Who Rode Away" is perhaps Lawrence's masterpiece in the
fabulous-symbolic kind, but it belongs more to his dealings with
the mythology of Mexico than to his stories as such. "The Princess"
can be fairly quickly dismissed. It is a product of the sort of doctrinaire
cruelty that possessed Lawrence for at least a part of this period; a
more distasteful variant of it is found in the later story "None of
That." . . . Yet there is something repellent about the treatment of
this story, as about the treatment of similar themes elsewhere in
Lawrence. I believe it is an impurity of motive, perceptible but hard
to pin down. Lawrence is often implicated in his stories in the wrong
way; and often he overcomes the difficulty by putting himself or a representative of himself into the fiction. This is not the most refined

artistic method, but as often as not it works. "The Princess" is handled differently. Romero's motive in the story is sexual revenge; and without admitting it, Lawrence seems to participate in this sentiment. He does not, it is true, sentimentalise Romero, who remains a most disagreeable specimen. But it is hard to get rid of the feeling that the author, not only his character, also wants to revenge himself on all cold white women, especially if they are rich; and it is this suspicion of a suppressed sexual malice in the tale, rather than the subject itself, that makes it offensive.

. . .

. . . [I]n turning to the stories of the last phase we are aware, for the most part, of an abrupt decline of seriousness and intensity. . . . The volume, including "The Woman Who Rode Away," published under this title in 1928, includes a number of post-Mexican stories, and it was the last collection to appear in Lawrence's lifetime. Several other stories were written about the same time for various periodicals, and they may all be dealt with together. Two new features become prominent in them—a strong element of personal satire and the use of the supernatural. Neither is particularly beneficial. As for the first, Lawrence had always used his friends and acquaintances, often too directly, as material for his works; but generally for some creative purpose. A real figure may have been used unscrupulously, but he takes his place in a pattern that goes beyond malicious portraiture. But in several of these late stories—"Smile," "Jimmy and the Desperate Woman," "The Man Who Loved Islands," "Things," perhaps others—the dominant motive seems to be irritation, contempt or amusement inspired purely by individual characters and their behaviour. Though the vigour and aptness of the writing is as great as ever, the effects are specialised and negative. The wine has gone thinner and sourer in the time from "The Fox" and "The Captain's Doll." And as for the supernatural, in "The Border Line," "The Last Laugh" and "Glad Ghosts" it becomes too easy an evasion of the storyteller's problem to work out a theme through the medium of character and action. Ghosts should be raised in fiction by people who believe in them or by those whose aim is to produce a shudder of the nerves. Lawrence belongs to neither of these classes, and his ghostly visitants only produce effects that in his more vigorous moods would have been achieved through the conflict of character and circumstance.

These qualifications do not deny the appearance of a hard, shrewd perception and an easy executive power. The opening description in

"Jimmy and the Desperate Woman" is a brilliant, acid piece of character-drawing.

. . .

And Jimmy's actual meeting with a hard-bitten miner's wife is a triumph of ironical imagination. The sardonic dexterity Lawrence shows here, and in "Things," for instance, would be the making of an ordinary satirist. But with him it is hard to avoid the feeling that an imagination meant for other ends is being used in an almost petulantly destructive way. Or, if more is attempted, it is not employed with sufficiently sustained intensity to penetrate the structure of the tale. This is the trouble with "The Border Line. " . . .

"Glad Ghosts" compels a similar judgement. . . . And as for "The Last Laugh," it describes one of those embarrassing visitations of Pan to Hampstead that illustrates emphatically the way not to evoke the chthonic powers. "The Rocking-Horse Winner" is an exception among the supernatural tales. It is not at all a Laurentian story—fancy rather than imagination—this tale of a small boy who by riding his toy rocking-horse can spot the winners of real races. The supernatural element is boldly and properly left unexplained, and is not made the substitute for a psychological reality that could be presented without it. The theme develops into a hectic and pathetic tale of gambling fever that destroys the boy himself as it reaches a successful climax; most skilfully done, but quite outside the range of Lawrence's usual work.

In other stories he is rather laboriously calling up old themes. "Sun" is a dreary tale of an unsatisfied American woman with a pallid business-man husband who finds a kind of fulfillment by living in Italy, sun-bathing all the time, and looking at a hard brown peasant. And "The Lovely Lady" returns to the equally worn subject of possessive maternity and frustrated manhood. In fact, in many of these stories Lawrence went nearer to popularising his gospel on the magazine-story level than he had ever done before. His energies were limited by illness; the best of them were absorbed by *Lady Chatterley* and exhausted by the subsequent controversy; so that the full force was rarely available to turn into the minor works.

Julian Moynahan

The common judgment that Lawrence's short stories and novellas contain a higher proportion of assured artistic successes than do his novels is substantially correct. One knows how to restore the faith of a reader who has bogged down halfway through *The Plumed Serpent* or fainted amid the profuse incremental repetitions of *The Rainbow*. Send him to "The Fox" or "Daughters of the Vicar" or "The Prussian Officer" or even "The Captain's Doll," and watch the brightness flow back into his eyes. Certainly, Lawrence is a great writer of the shorter tale, and if he is less than Chekov he still has no equal among English writers, who have failed, by and large, to make their mark in this form. When we think of the modern short story in English we remember Hemingway and Joyce, perhaps Faulkner, Fitzgerald, Katherine Anne Porter, and Sean O'Faolain. But the scope, originality, and poise of Lawrence's stories establish him as a more considerable figure than any of these non-English writers, and this is worth emphasizing, since, in a purely insular context, Lawrence's title to pre-eminence is apt to be conferred by an embarrassing default.

And yet, this is not to suggest that Lawrence's shorter fiction taken as a whole is more valuable than his work in the novel. Literary value is determined not only by the achievements of formal discipline but also by the scale and size of what is attempted and done. Lawrence's ten novels are in the nature of a continuous speculation or experiment. He is constantly pushing beyond old limits, with respect to both feeling and form. As he alternately gropes and races toward radically new conclusions he is like an explorer who must move tirelessly across his newly discovered territory in order to establish its extent and claim it for his own. Once crossed and claimed the land becomes amenable to settlement, domestication, and finely scaled map-making. If the novels are Lawrence's major exploration of human reality,

From *The Deed of Life: The Novels and Tales of D. H. Lawrence*. Princeton, N.J.: Princeton University Press, 1963. © 1991 by Julian Moynahan. Reprinted by permission of Julian Moynahan.

his lonely and at times heroic (and at times murky) vision of a land unknown, the tales represent just such settlement and domestication. They fill in behind the advancing frontier and turn virgin land into neighborhoods.

There is no doubt that the shorter fiction contains less strained argument and fewer lapses into uncertainty or confusion; that Lawrence was frequently able to effect a more direct release of his peculiarly rich sense of life within "disciplined limits"; that he moved easily within those limits whether he had in hand a mere sketch of half a dozen pages or a near novel like "St. Mawr." Nevertheless, we need to make certain discriminations: to set aside the work that is merely good, or primarily interesting in its relation to Lawrence's autobiography or to his doctrines, in order to appreciate how much remains that is great and unique.

As one reads through the three volumes of short stories and the two volumes of short novels in the Phoenix Edition it is rather easy to group many of the tales according to reasonably distinct categories; yet, as might be expected, it is the best work that finally eludes the simple category. One group can be put together from the several stories which read as suggestive footnotes to certain of the novels. The most weirdly interesting of these is the early "The Shades of Spring," describing the return to his home valley of one John Syson, a young man who, like Paul Morel, had courted and then left a girl living on a farm. . . . "Shades of Spring" is a kind of arch which ties together the erotic dilemma of *Sons and Lovers* and the final solution of the dilemma in *Lady Chatterley*. We may want to conclude that Lawrence, after all, had only one story to tell, which he went on reworking until the ending came right, but a more reasonable inference is that the Miriam figure was from the beginning much more a plastic imaginative construct than a mere travesty of Lawrence's childhood sweetheart Jessie Chambers.

A second category, consisting of a half dozen or so stories that make fun of or otherwise discomfit certain people in the Lawrence circle, may be passed by quickly. "None of That" travesties Mabel Dodge's lust for willed experience and imagines a more sordid outcome to her career than the actual tough-minded woman would ever have tolerated. No less than four stories—"Smile," "The Border Line," "Jimmy and the Desperate Woman," and "The Last Laugh"—are aimed with some malice at J. Middleton Murry, the man to whom Lawrence most frequently assigned the role of Judas in the tragi-comedy of his relations with friends. "Things" distressed the American expatriate couple Earl and Achsah Brewster by exposing the materialism implicit in American upper-bohemian veneration of European antiquity, but these kind people still managed to remain on good terms with Lawrence to the very end of his life.

A third category consists of a few works of substantial length which remain ambitious failures, owing either to excessive schematism in the ideas underlying the story, or indifferent success in the attempt to represent fictionally states of being about which Lawrence was confused or perverse. "The Ladybird" (*pace* Dr. Leavis) is, stylistically, Lawrence's ugliest story....

"The Woman Who Rode Away," although it contains some of Lawrence's most brilliant renderings of landscape, is, like *The Plumed Serpent,* a heartless tale *au fond.* Both the Woman and Constance Chatterley "throw themselves away," the latter in the direction of renewed life, the former merely into an abyss of senseless blood sacrifice. The Woman's ritual disembowelment by Mexican Indians seeking to recover the power of command they have lost to gringos is neither excusable nor interesting; and the story contains one of the most depressing images in all Lawrence: a blonde woman crawling on hands and knees along a narrow mountain ledge, while her two Indian captors walk easily erect, one before, one behind, both indifferent to her discomfort and danger.

"The Man Who Died" is a near-success until the baroque conceit of "I am risen!" destroys the suspension of disbelief required for Lawrence's bold attempt to merge his own and the Christian myth of bodily resurrection. Analogous difficulties crop up in a spirit story like "Glad Ghosts." The lady ghost here remains too involved in problems of the life of the senses to persuade us that she is as other-worldly as the convention demands. She is apt to remind the reader of the last, unfinished canto of Byron's *Don Juan,* where Juan mistakes for a phanton a warm, nubile lady wearing a sheet.

One of the most clear-cut groups among Lawrence's short stories consists of "Two Blue Birds," "The Lovely Lady," "Mother and Daughter," "Rawdon's Roof," and "The Blue Moccasins." These are united by their rather bitchy, facetious tone. The characters are middle- and upper-middle-class English people, and a recurring figure in several of these stories is the strong-minded, aging woman who has fastened herself parasitically onto someone younger and less clever than herself. Without abandoning his characteristic concern for vitality Lawrence successfully exploits here a talent for comedy of manners which he rarely employs in his novels. There is nothing to urge against these stories except that they are a bit too brittle and slight compared to his best work.

I could continue this categorizing—for example, the early stories of working-class life, the three thoroughly unsuccessful stories about sexual conflict set in or near London and obviously written during Lawrence's first years in London ("The Old Adam," "The Witch A La Mode," "New Eve and Old Adam")—except that I am much less interested in my schemes as such than to suggest what a large body of first-rate work remains after the ground has been cleared of work that is merely interesting, flawed, or only good enough to have made the international reputation of a lesser writer. . . .

In the short story Lawrence's finest achievements are: "Odour of Chrysanthemums," "The Prussian Officer," "The Thorn in the Flesh," "Daughters of the Vicar," "The Shadow in the Rose Garden," "The Blind Man," "The Horse-Dealer's Daughter," "The Princess" (a marginal case), "The Man Who Loved Islands," "The Rocking-Horse Winner." And among the short novels the best are: "Love Among the Haystacks," "The Fox," "The Captain's Doll," "St. Mawr" (another marginal case), "The Virgin and the Gypsy." By calling these Lawrence's best tales I mean to place them on a par with, say, "Byezhin Meadow," "In the Ravine," "The Death of Ivan Ilych," "A Simple Heart," "The Dead," "Bartleby the Scrivener," "Young Goodman Brown," and "The Light of the World." . . .

Julian Moynahan

Lawrence's ways of writing a story are not very imitable. Without the animating power of his vision the would-be disciple is apt to produce overblown lyricism, realism run to seed in lushness, hapless parody, or soft-core pornography. The modern realistic story, with its managed point of view and spare use of what Ford called "telling details" is, on the contrary, perfectly imitable. It can even be taught in creative-writing classes, as the late Frank O'Connor used to teach students in the Harvard Summer School to write Hemingway stories, Chekhov stories, and O'Connor stories. Has Lawrence then any followers? And what is the extent of his influence on writers coming after him?

I think the answer is that Lawrence had had [sic] few close followers—the American novelist and short-story writer Sherwood Anderson tried to strike the Laurentian note in some of his later work and the results were disastrous—but that his influence has been inescapable and pervasive. He has shown all later writers something fundamental: new forms can be generated through the freeing of feeling, yet this is a process requiring a very arduous discipline, the discipline of utter emotional honesty. Like all lessons offered by the masters it may take more than a lifetime to grasp. Nevertheless writers as far apart as Saul Bellow and George Orwell, Bernard Malamud and the Australian Patrick White, William Faulkner and Norman Mailer, Flannery O'Connor and Tillie Olsen, could not have moved as freely and adventurously in their artistic pursuits as they did and do had not Lawrence preceded them with his major breakthrough.

The literary future belongs to the young and the unborn. If they forget Lawrence they will be forgetting more than they can ever learn.

From the "Foreword" to Julian Moynahan's edition of *A Modern Lover and Other Stories* by D. H. Lawrence. New York: Ballantine Books, 1969. © 1969 by Julian Moynahan. Reprinted by permission of Julian L. Moynahan.

Ronald P. Draper

Lawrence's tales are an important part of his total work.... The stories themselves are of widely differing kinds. Some, like "Strike Pay" or "Two Blue Birds," are mere sketches; others—most notably, "Daughters of the Vicar," "The Fox," "The Captain's Doll," "St. Mawr," and "The Virgin and the Gipsy"—are short novels. Some are primarily realistic vignettes, and at the opposite extreme from these are tales which are virtually poems in prose: "Sun," "The Woman Who Rode Away," and "The Escaped Cock." Behind some of the tales there is a genuinely creative impulse—and, where these tales are concerned, it is possible to agree with those critics who find Lawrence aesthetically purer and more satisfying in the stories than in the novels. But others seem to be more potboilers or, at best, overspills from the experience that goes more completely into the novels. Lawrence seems never to have considered the short story seriously as a form. There are no new and striking critical pronouncements on it as there are on the novel in his letters and articles, or on poetry in his prefaces. It is true that he rarely engages in that direct lecturing of his readers which can be so irritating in the novels; it is as if he realizes that the shorter form cannot afford such dilution.... It is also true that some experimentation takes place in the tales, chiefly in the "poems in prose." But the virtues of most of the tales are those of the novels. The same kind of inspiration and the same manner of writing are evident in both.

From *D. H. Lawrence*. New York: Twayne, 1964, 119–20. Reprinted with permission of Twayne Publishers, Inc., an imprint of Macmillan Publishing Company. Copyright © 1964 by Twayne Publishers, Inc.

Walter Allen

D. H. Lawrence saw himself primarily as a novelist but in fact expressed himself in almost all the literary forms current in his time and with the like distinction in each, although it has been argued that in fiction he was best in the short story. . . .

I am not at all certain of this. The value of a literary work rests ultimately on something beyond method and technique which we can only call, clumsily, depth of insight. Lawrence, whatever form he chose to write in, was of a piece, no writer more so, and he wrote novels and stories side by side throughout the twenty-five years, more or less, of his writing life. However closely related, the novels and stories are not in competition with each other. As a short-story writer, though they are so different in kind that comparison between them would seem absurd, Lawrence, it seems to me, must be judged second only to Kipling in English writing.

His first volume, *The Prussian Officer*, appeared in 1914. F. R. Leavis, who has done so much for the recognition of Lawrence as a master of the short story, finds the title-story characterized by an "unpleasant kind of power." But this is inseparable from his genius, and although "The Prussian Officer" may be unpleasant, it is not uncharacteristic. Lawrence's customary theme is that of relationship and what it may symbolize; "The Prussian Officer" treats of the relationship between a professional soldier, a cavalry captain, and his conscript orderly. . . . The story is a daring dramatization of abnormal psychology. It is as much a "thought-adventure," to use his own phrase, as his novels. As such, it reminds me of another of his stories; I refer to "The Woman Who Rode Away," probably Lawrence's most remarkable and convincing rendering of the religious values of the Mexican Indians, a triumph of the empathetic imagination. . . .

From *The Short Story in English* by Walter Allen. Oxford: Oxford University Press, 1981, 99–109. Copyright © 1981 by Walter Allen. Reprinted by permission of Oxford University Press, Inc., and by permission of David Higham Associates.

"The Woman Who Rode Away," as Leavis says, "imagines the old pagan Mexican religion as something real and living," and Lawrence transmits his sense of this reality and vitality to the reader. The story is the fine fruit of Lawrence's experience of Mexico and also his astonishing ability to translate into imaginative reality the works of anthropology that he is known to have been reading at the time.

"The Woman Who Rode Away" is, of course, fully mature Lawrence. This "The Prussian Officer" may not be, but what cannot be disputed is the quality of the writing. Witness the first paragraph, which, without introducing either the captain or the orderly, frames the action. . . . It is a good example of Lawrence's prose, with its strong and subtle rhythms, its careful and cunningly placed verbal repetitions, its empathy into physical experience.

And the two short stories, for all their differences, have one thing in common very rare in short stories. They are conceived "from an enormous height," as Forster said of Hardy's novels. This means that though there are large areas of Lawrence's characters of which we know nothing, yet we do know enough about them for them to be able to take on the proportions of potentially tragic figures. Their individuality, their idiosyncrasy, may be stripped away; because of that, they remain fundamentally human.

This is apparent even in Lawrence's first accepted, though not first published, short story, "Odour of Chrysanthemums," which appeared in Ford Madox Hueffer's *English Review* in June 1911. It was collected in *The Prussian Officer,* and it may be useful to quote the first paragraph: [he quotes the first paragraph.] No need to comment on the quality of the prose or the author's acute perception of detail; every word carries weight.

My immediate reason for quoting the passage is to indicate that most of the stories in *The Prussian Officer* are products of Lawrence's day-to-day experience in the Nottinghamshire and Derbyshire coalfield. The first paragraph of the story might be thought to be slow, since we are always being told about the necessity of speed in the opening of a story. But beside setting the scene and giving us information which we shall recognize is crucially important, it is plainly conceived to distance the events of the story; it is one way by which Lawrence can be seen to be creating from an enormous height. . . .

What might be called the local stories in *The Prussian Officer* include two other of Lawrence's finest stories. Very different in manner and

147

content, they indicate something of the extent of his range. *The White Stocking* is a story of a young husband's discovery that his pretty little wife has been accepting presents from her former employer. It is a story of jealousy and reconciliation; we are convinced of the husband and the wife's love for each other. We are convinced, too, that the young woman means no harm: she cannot resist pretty things, tributes to her sexual attractiveness. It is a wonderful portrait of a flirtatious young woman unaware, perhaps, that her behaviour could be misconstrued, since for her it exists on the level of play. The story, it seems to me, can be compared only with Chekhov, with such a story as "The Darling."

"The Daughters of the Vicar" is the first version of a theme that Lawrence was many times to dramatize, the theme of upper-class sterility and the saving of an upper-class woman by the vitality and superior human values of a working man. . . .

Although Lawrence spent years of his literary life in near poverty, his genius was early and widely recognized, so that he was soon moving in social circles far removed from those of a miner's son at Eastwood and an elementary school teacher at Croydon. The range of scene and class dealt with in the novels and stories after the very early fiction was greatly expanded, and this was reinforced by the circumstances of his life from 1919 onwards, when he became a wanderer over the face of the earth. So in some sense the stories change. Often they become less obviously realistic. Sometimes they take the form of what one can only call fable, as in "The Man Who Loved Islands," which F. R. Leavis brilliantly relates to "Hawthorne's kind of fable, which is psychological, moral and philosophical." The man in question is a man in search of self-sufficiency who progresses, or deteriorates, from island to island, each further removed from human contact, until he ends his life alone on a bare rock in the Atlantic.

I have called the story a fable, but no moral is deduced or appended. It is not necessary that it should be, for it cannot be stressed too much that Lawrence's moral, for he was always a moralist, is there in the texture of the prose, the wonderful evocations, visualized in all their detail, of the islands the man inhabits.

More often, the later stories are extremely penetrating studies of character, as in "Jimmy and the Desperate Woman." . . .

"Jimmy and the Desperate Woman" is a story of great subtlety. Throughout, the tone of the narration is sardonic. In part, the story is about the old division in England between the north and the south, and the south is seen in some sense as an intruder, as Jimmy is between the Pinnegars. It is also about the exposure of a man who is governed by an inescapable impulse to dramatize himself and who cannot resist the temptation to experiment with his own feelings and with those of others, a man, one might say, who is congenitally incapable of sincerity, a man who also perhaps confuses life and literature. Lawrence does not need to tell us what the consequences of this particular action of Jimmy's will be. He is self-doomed, and we know he will glory in self-destruction.

In his last years, Lawrence wrote a number of stories which one can only call supernatural, since they describe events that are inexplicable. They carry the greater conviction because Lawrence makes no attempt to explain them. Among them are "Glad Ghosts," "The Last Laugh," and "The Rocking-Horse Winner," which is the most remarkable.

Brian Finney

1907–1914: The Formative Years

As a literary form the short story has a long history. But it was not until the late nineteenth century that it acquired the psychological subtlety and open-endedness that helped it to become a major fictional mode of the twentieth century. One of its greatest practitioners was D. H. Lawrence. To follow the development of his stories from the gauche anecdotes of his early twenties to the sophisticated parodies of the genre that he wrote in the last years of his life is like retracing the history of the genre from its pre-Chekovian social realism and watching it reach forward to the verbal play and self-conscious artifice of post-Modernist writers such as Borges and Beckett.

Like many of his fellow Modernists, Lawrence was self-taught. Ford Madox Ford reckoned that he had "never known any young man who was so well read in all the dullnesses that spread between Milton and George Eliot."[1] The first stories that he wrote in 1907 for a competition in his local newspaper are sentimental, heavily plotted and psychologically naive. During the following seven years he patiently wrote, rewrote and revised his stories to force them to accommodate his maturing vision of modern life. Plot becomes subordinated to urgent thematic impulses which require new modes of narrative expression. For instance, he completely transformed "The White Stocking," which he first wrote in 1907 as a fictionalized account of an embarrassing incident that happened to his mother in her youth. Over the next seven years he painfully reshaped it into a subtle psychological portrayal of the dramatic conflict between love and desire, ending in a release of emotion that undercuts the very medium he is using—verbal communication. This oblique focus on the ineffectuality of language, a language which is simultaneously being used to tell the story, is quintessentially Modernist.

From "Introduction" to *D. H. Lawrence, Selected Short Stories* (Penguin, 1982), 11–29. Copyright © 1982 by Brian Finney. Reprinted by permission of Brian Finney.

What had happened during those seven years? In the first place Lawrence was learning to replace literary models from the past with his own voice expressing his own convictions, among them the conviction that emotion and sensation are more powerful, if unconscious, psychological forces than reason and intellect. It is man's "passionate sub-conscious," he wrote later, "which makes the story," not "the mechanical upper half."[2] This belief led to a search for a more satisfactory form than the rigid closed structure he had inherited from the Edwardian generation of writers, Bennett, Galsworthy, and Wells. Their tight rules of construction reflected the tightly structured society of their England.

But once the power of the unconscious to shape man's destiny is given proper recognition a new form is needed to accommodate its less predictable operations. As Lawrence was to observe in his introduction to a collection of Giovanni Verga's short stories: "The emotional mind, however apparently muddled, has its own rhythms, [*sic*—Lawrence wrote "rhythm"] its own commas and colons and full-stops."[3] What was needed, Lawrence decided, was a looser narrative form altogether: "We need an apparent formlessness, definite form is mechanical."[4] For this reason he even turned his back on Henry James, himself a precursor of Modernism, because, as Lawrence saw it, "subtle conventional design was his aim."[5] In other words James had only modified his predecessors' obsession for artistic form. Whereas for Lawrence "a great deal of the meaning of life and of art lies in the apparently dull spaces, the pauses, the unimportant passages."[6] During Lawrence's formative period between 1907 and 1914 the gradual subordination of plot to thematic considerations is accompanied by a jettisoning of conventional form for an apparent formlessness that reflects the irrational movements of the unconscious psyche.

Of course it would be wrong to suggest that Lawrence replaced the nineteenth century's reliance on man's mental abilities by a Freudian advocacy of the superiority of the unconscious. Between 1907 and 1914 Lawrence was evolving a dualistic vision of man which recognized the need to balance intellect against emotion, and reason against feeling. Because he became especially aware of the imbalance into which man had been thrown by the Industrial Revolution, he appears to celebrate the life of the passions at the expense of the more conscious life of the mind. In fact he is only trying to redress the balance. It is the underlying concern with life's dual nature which in-

forms the shape of his earlier stories—almost all of which were collected in *The Prussian Officer* in 1914. One has only to think of the closing tableaux of the two lovers restored by touch to the source of their
true passion in "The White Stocking," or of the dead bodies of the
officer and his orderly laid out side by side in the title story, to see how
positive and negative instances of life's essential duality provide both
the matter and the shape of these stories.

The first eight stories in this selection all belong to this first phase
in Lawrence's life. All were rewritten or drastically revised between
1913 and 1914. Because he forgot about it, "Love Among the Haystacks," which dates from 1913, shows Lawrence still clinging to some
of the pre-Modernist insistence on plot (especially in its over-tidy
happy ending) that has been shed in the remaining seven stories—all
of which were revised in 1914 for inclusion in *The Prussian Officer*. Yet
already the need to strike an equipoise between the polarized attitudes which each of the brothers in this story displays simultaneously
provides it with artistic shape. . . .

This need to achieve a balance between conscious and unconscious
forces in the human psyche lies at the root of all these early stories,
and many of the later ones too. Yet the fact remains that Lawrence is
still largely unaware of the philosophical basis underpinning the
fiction of this period. Each new story is a separate exploration of a
unique situation—one, moreover, which is frequently developed from
an incident in his own life or in the lives of those close to him. A comparison of the different versions of these earlier stories shows among
other things how rapidly he acquired the ability to transform the raw
material of life into the detached vision of the self-critical artist.

. . .

Artistic criticism and self-criticism inform one another at this period
of Lawrence's career. Perhaps the clearest example of this process is
the evolution of "The Shades of Spring" from "A Modern Lover.". . .
By attending closely to the probabilities within his fictive models
Lawrence has been brought to realize that his earlier fictional embod-
iments of Jessie were distortions produced by his need for self-
justification. The writing of the successive versions of this story
were—even more than in the case of *Sons and Lovers*—therapeutic
acts for the man as much as the artist.

Further evidence of the advances that Lawrence was making in
purely literary terms during this period appears in the growing

confidence with which he employs metaphor and symbol. Touch and sight in particular are used by him in a wide variety of situations to represent the battle raging between conscious and unconscious forces within his different characters. Touch connects them to one another's deepest emotional currents, while sight often signifies the penetrating impact of the intellect. . . .

Lawrence's use of complex symbolism has become equally sophisticated during this period. Sometimes he introduces it with the lightest of touches, as is the case with the chrysanthemums in "Odour of Chrysanthemums" or the distant mountains in "The Prussian Officer." . . . In at least one story, "Second Best," symbolism is employed as the dominant narrative mode. . . .

Immediately after Frances has witnessed the death of the mole the glittering landscape loses its magic for her, seeming "scarcely worth the notice." But in the next two paragraphs Lawrence takes care to reaffirm the beauty of the surrounding countryside. This use of nature as a norm against which characters can be implicitly judged by the reader without interference from the author occurs repeatedly in the stories of this time. . . .

To rely on any form of external prop for one's deepest satisfaction is fatal in Lawrence's view, whether the prop is the armed forces, as is the case with Bachmann [in "The Thorn in the Flesh"] and with Alfred in "Daughters of the Vicar," class, as it is with the Lindleys, or morality as it is with the Lindley's daughter, Mary, both in the latter story. . . . [several sentences on "Daughters of the Vicar"]

1915–1922: The War Years and Their Aftermath

. . . This formulation of his metaphysic [that Lawrence articulated in writing his "Study of Thomas Hardy" and "The Crown"] necessarily affected the nature of the stories he wrote over the next seven years, 1915 to 1922. All eight stories in this selection emanating from this middle period and collected (with one exception) in *England, My England* (1922) show a new awareness of the wider significance of individual characters' actions and behavior. Most of the stories reflect the destructive spirit finding such monstrous expression in the battlefields of France. But, with the exception of "England, My England," the stories concentrate on individuals at home warring with themselves and one another. Lawrence is more interested in analyzing individual self-destruction than the mass destruction it produced.

. . . .

The formulation of a metaphysic allowed Lawrence to write about a wide variety of domestic situations in such a way that they reflected the schizophrenic condition of his war-torn society. . . .

In concentrating on the war at home many of the stories of this period focus on the war between the sexes. Both "England, My England" and "The Mortal Coil" establish a causal link between sexual and military warfare. A further three stories represent the hero as a male predator ruthlessly seeking out his mate in defiance of norms of social behavior ["You Touched Me," "Samson and Delilah," and "Tickets, Please"].

. . .

This use of a classical parallel in "Tickets, Please" and of biblical models in "Samson and Delilah" and "The Horse-Dealer's Daughter" goes hand in hand with a more confident use of comedy. All three stories open on a comic note and normally modulate into a more serious tone towards the end. In "Fanny and Annie," however, Lawrence makes sustained use of comedy throughout. . . . [two paragraphs on "Fanny and Annie"]

. . . .

1923–1928: A Period of Formal Experimentation

Lawrence continued to extend and refine his philosophical system in various essays written between 1917 and 1921. As he grew more assertive about what he called his "pollyanalytics" he was compelled to search for new narrative forms that lent themselves more readily to the expression of an ever-widening set of associated concepts. The need to link the actions of individuals to larger historical, social, political, and religious forces led him to reject the more naturalistic narrative modes of his youth in favor of literary forms traditionally open to symbolic interpretation. In this final period he reaches new heights of formal inventiveness, experimenting with genres like myth, the fairy story and satiric comedy—all of which traditionally present individuals as representative of universal patterns of behavior. Or he makes use of conventional literary forms like the ghost story and the murder story only to break their mechanistic rules and reverse the reader's normal expectations.

Two of the stories in this collection show Lawrence turning to primitive myths in which the heroine is confronted with the natural world from which she and her kind have become dangerously alienated. "The Woman Who Rode Away" offers a negative vision of the fatal consequences of such alienation; "Sun," on the other hand, offers a positive example of a woman restored to the cosmos and to health. . . .

In his flight from realistic narrative modes, Lawrence made a number of forays into the traditionally escapist genres of the ghost story and the murder story. Yet invariably he turns the conventions of each genre upside down. His ghosts, spirits of the dead, show more life than the living who have themselves become "ghosts" in Lawrence's redefinition of the term. Similarly murder, Lawrence explained in his essay on Edgar Allan Poe, need not entail physical death for the victim, who can continue to live "in the post-mortem reality, a living dead."[7] Drawing on the tradition of the psychological ghost and murder story established by Henry James, Lawrence forces his readers to abandon the imaginary world of Gothic horror and underground vaults for the reality of "that which takes place beneath the consciousness."[8]

. . . .

Lawrence was well aware of the mechanistic nature of the conventional murder story and criticized Poe for turning his characters into mere automatons. In the same essay he redefined murder in psychological terms as "a lust to get at the very quick of life itself, and kill it."[9] Using this radically new definition he is able to restore to the murder story the emotional and psychological interest which the genre traditionally excludes.

. . . .

"The Man Who Loved Islands" echoes "The Rocking-Horse Winner" when it begins with the traditional opening line of a fairy tale, only omitting the "Once upon a time." Cathcart, the protagonist of this story, is at first called "the Master," then "the islander," finally simply "he." Throughout this moral fable of our time Lawrence maintains a stance of comic detachment. . . . It is a beautifully controlled allegory in which the medium happily accommodates the message.

The other major literary mode which Lawrence explored in these final years is that of satiric comedy, a natural development from his earlier use of pure comedy. At this time he was waging almost incessant war on the shibboleths of western society, much in the same way as the satirists of pre-Christian times used their formidable magic powers of invective against their society's enemies. The major difference between Lawrence and these originators of the genre is that his enemies were actually the pillars of society. "Satire," wrote Lawrence, "exists for the very purpose of killing the social being, showing him what an inferior he is and, with all his parade of social honesty, how subtly and corruptly debased."[10] Three stories exemplify this vein of satire: ["Jimmy and the Desperate Woman," "Things," and "Mother and Daughter"]. . . .

Notes

1. E. Nehls, *D. H. Lawrence: A Composite Biography*, 3 vols. (University of Wisconsin Press, 1957–59), Vol. I, p. 116.

2. *The Collected Letters of D. H. Lawrence*, 2 vols., ed. H. T. Moore (Heinemann, 1962), pp. 841, 852. [Lawrence says "mechanical upper self"; see *Letters*, V, 294.]

3. *Phoenix: The Posthumous Papers of D. H. Lawrence*, ed. E. D. McDonald (Heinemann, 1936), p. 250.

4. ibid., p. 248.

5. *Collected Letters*, op. cit., p. 388.

6. *Phoenix*, op. cit., p. 248.

7. *The Symbolic Meaning*, ed. Armin Arnold (Centaur Press, 1962), 107.

8. *Studies in Classic American Literature* (Penguin Books, 1971), p. 85.

9. ibid., p. 86.

10. *Phoenix*, op. cit., p. 453. [I can find no such passage.]

Chronology

Unless otherwise indicated, dates for works are dates of publication.

1885 David Herbert Lawrence born 11 September, in Eastwood, Nottinghamshire, England.

1901 Leaves Nottingham High School.

1907 "A Prelude" (story) published in *Nottinghamshire Guardian.*

1908 Begins teaching at Davidson Road School, Croyden.

1910 Mother dies on 9 December. "Goose Fair" (short story) published in the *English Review.*

1911 Stricken by pneumonia in November; *The White Peacock* (first novel; published in January).

1912 In February resigns his teaching position; in March meets and falls in love with Frieda von Richthofen Weekley; in May goes to the continent with her. *The Trespasser* (novel).

1913 *Love Poems and Others; Sons and Lovers* (novel).

1914 *The Widowing of Mrs. Holroyd* (play); revises short stories for book publication as *The Prussian Officer and Other Stories.*

1915 *The Rainbow* (novel) published and suppressed by authorities.

1916 *Twilight in Italy* (travel); *Amores* (poems).

1917 *Look! We Have Come Through!* (poems).

1918 *New Poems.*

1919 Leaves England for Italy, then Capri and Sicily. *Bay: A Book of Poems.*

1920 *Touch and Go* (play); *Women in Love* (novel); *The Lost Girl* (novel).

1921 *Movements in European History* (history text, published under the pseudonym Lawrence H. Davison); *Psychoanalysis and the Unconscious* (essay in psychology); *Tortoises* (six poems); *Sea and Sardinia* (travel).

1922 With Frieda leaves Italy for Ceylon; spends May through August in Australia; arrives in California in September and proceeds to New Mexico. *Aaron's Rod* (novel); *Fantasia of the Unconscious* (essay in psychology); *England, My England* (short stories).

1923 In Mexico and the United States until November, when he sails for England. *The Ladybird* (U.S. title *The Captain's Doll*) (three novellas); *Studies in Classic American Literature* (literary criticism); *Kangaroo* (novel); *Birds, Beasts and Flowers* (poems).

1924 Travels in England, France, and Germany until March, when he sails for New York; travels in United States and Mexico. *The Boy in the Bush* (novel, written jointly with Mollie L. Skinner).

1925 Continues to travel and reside in Mexico and the United States until September, when he sails for England; briefly in England, then on to Germany and Italy. *St. Mawr, together with The Princess* (novella and long story); *Reflections on the Death of a Porcupine and Other Essays* (seven essays).

1926 Moves about in Italy, France, Great Britain, and Germany. *The Plumed Serpent* (novel); *David* (play).

1927 *Mornings in Mexico* (travel).

1928 Leaves Italy for Switzerland in January; to the French riviera in October. *The Woman Who Rode Away and Other Stories* (10 stories; 11 in U.S. ed.); *Lady Chatterley's Lover* (novel); *The Collected Poems of D. H. Lawrence*.

1929 *The Paintings of D. H. Lawrence; Pansies* (poems); *The Escaped Cock* (novella).

1930 Dies at Vence, France, on 2 March.

Bibliography

Primary Works

Most of Lawrence's works were published both in London and in New York; publication information is usually given only for whichever edition appeared first. For full publication information, see Warren Roberts, *A Bibliography of D.H. Lawrence*, 2d ed. (1982).

Collections of Short Stories and Novellas
Most of Lawrence's stories were published in magazines before book publication; see Roberts's *Bibliography* for details.

The Complete Short Stories of D.H. Lawrence. 3 vols. London: William Heinemann, 1955. Forty-seven stories.

"England, My England" and Other Stories. New York: Thomas Seltzer, 1922. Ten stories: "England, My England," "Tickets, Please," "The Blind Man," "Monkey Nuts," "Wintry Peacock," "You Touched Me," "Samson and Delilah," "The Primrose Path," "The Horse-Dealer's Daughter," and "Fanny and Annie."

The Escaped Cock. Paris: Black Sun Press, 1929. Novella—subsequently entitled "The Man Who Died." (New edition with apparatus edited by Gerald M. Lacy, 1973.)

The Ladybird. London: Martin Secker, 1923. Three novellas: "The Ladybird," "The Fox," and "The Captain's Doll." (Published in the United States as *The Captain's Doll*.)

"Love Among the Haystacks" and Other Pieces. London: Nonesuch Press, 1930. Four Stories or sketches: "Love Among the Haystacks," "A Chapel Among the Mountains," "A Hay Hut Among the Mountains," and "Once." (U.S. edition [October 1933] also contains "Christs in the Tirol.")

The Lovely Lady. London: Martin Secker, 1933. Eight stories: "The Lovely Lady," "Rawdon's Roof," "The Rocking-Horse Winner," "Mother and Daughter," "The Blue Moccasins," "Things," "The Overtone," and "The Man Who Loved Islands."

A Modern Lover. London: Martin Secker, 1934. Seven stories: "A Modern Lover," "The Old Adam," "Her Turn," "Strike Pay," "The Witch a la Mode," "New Eve and Old Adam," and "Mr. Noon."

Bibliography

"The Prussian Officer" and Other Stories. London: Duckworth and Co., 1914. Twelve stories: "The Prussian Officer," "The Thorn in the Flesh," "Daughters of the Vicar," "A Fragment of Stained Glass," "The Shades of Spring," "Second Best," "The Shadow in the Rose Garden," "Goose Fair," "The White Stocking," "A Sick Collier," "The Christening," and "Odour of Chrysanthemums."

The Short Novels. 2 vols. London: William Heinemann, 1956. Seven short novels: "Love Among the Haystacks," "The Ladybird," "The Fox," "The Captain's Doll," "St. Mawr," "The Virgin and the Gipsy," and "The Man Who Died."

"St. Mawr," together with "The Princess." London: Martin Secker, 1925. Novella and long short story. (U.S. edition did not include "The Princess.")

The Tales of D. H. Lawrence. London: Martin Secker, 1934. Collects all of the stories and novellas previously published in the four story collections and in *The Ladybird; "St. Mawr," together with "The Princess;" The Escaped Cock;* and *The Virgin and the Gipsy.*

The Virgin and the Gipsy. Florence, Italy: G. Orioli, 1930. Novella, published from Lawrence's unrevised manuscript.

"The Woman Who Rode Away" and Other Stories. London: Martin Secker, 1928. Ten stories: "Two Blue Birds," "Sun," "The Woman Who Rode Away," "Smile," "The Border Line," "Jimmy and the Desperate Woman," "The Last Laugh," "In Love," "Glad Ghosts," and "None of That." (U.S. edition also includes "The Man Who Loved Islands.")

Novels

Aaron's Rod. New York: Thomas Seltzer, 1922.

The Boy in the Bush. (Written in collaboration with Mollie L. Skinner.) London: Martin Secker, 1924.

The First Lady Chatterley. New York: Dial Press, 1944. (The first of the three versions that Lawrence wrote.)

John Thomas and Lady Jane. (The second version of *Lady Chatterley's Lover.*) New York: Viking Press, 1972.

Kangaroo. London: Martin Secker, 1923.

Lady Chatterley's Lover. [Florence, Italy:] Privately printed, 1928; expurgated edition, London: Martin Secker, 1932.

The Lost Girl. London: Martin Secker, 1920.

The Plumed Serpent. London: Martin Secker, 1926.

The Rainbow. London: Methuen and Co., 1915.

Sons and Lovers. London: Duckworth and Co., 1913.

The Trespasser. London: Duckworth and Co., 1912.

The White Peacock. New York: Duffield and Co., 1911.

Women in Love. New York: Privately printed, 1920; London: Martin Secker, 1921.

Poems and Plays

Amores. London: Duckworth and Co., 1916. (Poems)
Bay: A Book of Poems. [London: Beaumont Press,] 1919.
Birds, Beasts and Flowers. New York: Thomas Seltzer, 1923. (Poems)
The Collected Poems of D. H. Lawrence. 2 vols. London: Martin Secker, 1928.
The Collier's Friday Night. London: Martin Secker, 1934. In *Complete Plays*, 469–530.
The Complete Plays of D. H. Lawrence. New York: Viking Press, 1966. Includes *The Widowing of Mrs. Holroyd, David, The Married Man, The Daughter-in-Law, The Fight for Barbara, Touch and Go, The Merry-Go-Round, A Collier's Friday Night,* and the fragments "Altitude," and "Noah's Flood."
Complete Poems. 3 vols. London: William Heinemann, 1957.
The Complete Poems of D. H. Lawrence. 2 vols. Edited with introduction and notes by V. de Sola Pinto and Warren Roberts. New York: Viking Press, 1964.
David. London: Martin Secker, 1926. In *Complete Plays*, 63–154.
Last Poems. Edited by Richard Aldington. Florence, Italy: G. Orioli, 1932.
Look! We Have Come Through! London: Chatto and Windus, 1917. (Poems)
Love Poems and Others. London: Duckworth and Co., 1913.
Nettles. London: Faber and Faber, 1930. (Poems)
New Poems. London: Martin Secker, 1918. (First U.S. edition, June 1920, contains a preface, "Poetry of the Present," by Lawrence.)
Pansies. London: Martin Secker, 1929. (Poems)
The Plays of D. H. Lawrence. London: Martin Secker, 1933. Three plays: *The Widowing of Mrs. Holroyd, Touch and Go,* and *David.* (All previously published)
Poems. 2 vols. London: William Heinemann, 1939. (First posthumous collected edition)
Tortoises. New York: Thomas Seltzer, 1921. (Poems)
Touch and Go. London: C. W. Daniel, 1920. In *Complete Plays*, 321–86.
The Widowing of Mrs. Holroyd. New York: Mitchell Kennerley, 1914. In *Complete Plays*, 9–61.

Miscellaneous Works

Apocalypse. Florence, Italy: G. Orioli, 1931. (Biblical exegisis)
Assorted Articles. London: Martin Secker, 1930. (Essays and newspaper articles; for a full list of contents, see Roberts's *Bibliography*)

Bibliography

The Collected Letters of D. H. Lawrence. 2 vols. Edited by Harry T. Moore. New York: Viking Press, 1962.

D. H. Lawrence: Letters to Thomas and Adele Seltzer. Edited by Gerald M. Lacy. Santa Barbara, Calif.: Black Sparrow Press, 1976.

Etruscan Places. London: Martin Secker, 1932. (Travel book)

Fantasia of the Unconscious. New York: Thomas Seltzer, 1922 (Essay in psychology)

The Letters of D. H. Lawrence. Edited with an introduction by Aldous Huxley. London: William Heinemann, 1932.

Mornings in Mexico. London: Martin Secker, 1927. (Travel book)

Movements in European History. London: Oxford University Press, 1921. (History text, published under the pseudonym Lawrence H. Davison) Illustrated edition, 1925; the 1971 Oxford edition prints the "Epilogue" for the first time.

The Paintings of D. H. Lawrence. London: Mandrake Press, 1929. (Includes an "Introduction" written by Lawrence)

Phoenix: The Posthumous Papers of D. H. Lawrence. Edited by Edward D. McDonald. New York: Viking Press, 1936. (Large collection of miscellaneous material—essays, reviews, sketches—some previously unpublished)

Phoenix II: Uncollected, Unpublished, and Other Prose Works by D. H. Lawrence. Edited by Warren Roberts and Harry T. Moore. New York: Viking Press, 1968. (Stories, sketches, reviews, essays, some previously unpublished or uncollected; also contains all of *Reflections on the Death of a Porcupine* and *Assorted Articles*)

Psychoanalysis and the Unconscious. New York: Thomas Seltzer, 1921. (Essay in psychology)

Reflections on the Death of a Porcupine and Other Essays. Philadelphia: Centaur Press, 1925. Seven essays: "The Crown," "The Novel," "Him with His Tail in His Mouth," "Blessed Are the Powerful," "Love Was Once a Little Boy," "Reflections on the Death of a Porcupine," and "Aristocracy."

Sea and Sardina. New York: Thomas Seltzer, 1921. (Travel book)

Studies in Classic American Literature. New York: Thomas Seltzer, 1923. (Literary criticism)

The Symbolic Meaning: The Uncollected Versions of Studies in Classic American Literature. Edited by Armin Arnold, with a Preface by Harry T. Moore. N.P.: Centaur Press, 1962; New York: Viking Press, 1964.

Twilight in Italy. London: Duckworth and Co., 1916. (Travel book)

Cambridge University Press is publishing a complete edition of Lawrence's works and his letters. The contents of some volumes of this new edition—especially those containing essays and short stories—do not replicate those of earlier volumes.

Secondary Works

This list includes those books, parts of books, and articles that discuss the stories in some generic way, or that deal with a number of the short stories: I have not included explications of individual stories. Readers of D. H. Lawrence are fortunate to have two extensive and reliable annotated bibliographies of material about D. H. Lawrence: James Cowan's *D. H. Lawrence: An Annotated Bibliography of Writings About Him*, 2 vols. (De Kalb: Northern Illinois University Press, 1982, 1984), and Thomas Jackson Rice's *D. H. Lawrence: A Guide to Research* (New York: Garland, 1983). The cut-off date for the Cowan volumes is 1975, and for Rice's it is 1983. More recent material on the short stories can be found in the annual bibliographies in *PMLA* (analyzed by individual story), in the fall issue of the *D. H. Lawrence Review*, and in *Studies in Short Fiction*.

Allen, Walter. *The Short Story in English*. Oxford: Clarendon Press, 1981.

Amon, Frank. "D. H. Lawrence and the Short Story." In *The Achievement of D. H. Lawrence*, edited by Frederick J. Hoffman and Harry T. Moore. Norman: University of Oklahoma Press, 1953.

Bates, H. E. "Lawrence and the Writers of Today." In *The Modern Short Story: A Critical Survey*. 1941; London: Michael Joseph, 1972.

Bayley, John. *The Short Story: Henry James to Elizabeth Bowen*. Brighton, England: Harvester Press, 1988.

Beachcroft, T. O. *The Modest Art: A Survey of the Short Story in English*. London: Oxford University Press, 1968.

Beal, Anthony. "Outside the Novels." In *D. H. Lawrence*, 98–110. New York: Grove Press, 1961.

Becker, George J. "Short Stories and Novellas." In *D. H. Lawrence*, 113–30. New York: Frederick Ungar, 1980.

Black, Michael. *D. H. Lawrence: The Early Fiction. A Commentary*. Cambridge: Cambridge University Press, 1986.

Blanchard, Lydia. "D. H. Lawrence." In *Critical Survey of Short Fiction*, 7 vols. edited by Frank N. Magill, 5:1788–94. Englewood Cliffs, N.J.: Salem Press, 1981.

———. "Lawrence on the Fighting Line: Changes in Form of the Post-War Short Fiction." *D.H. Lawrence Review* 16, no. 3 (Fall 1983): 235–46.

Brunsdale, Mitzi M. *The German Effect on D. H. Lawrence and His Works, 1885–1912*. Berne, Switzerland: Lang, 1978.

Burwell, Rose Marie. "A Checklist of Lawrence's Reading." In *A D. H. Lawrence Handbook*, edited by Keith Sagar, 59–125. New York: Barnes and Noble, 1982.

Bibliography

Clark, L. D. *The Minoan Distance: The Symbolism of Travel in D. H. Lawrence.* Tucson: University of Arizona Press, 1980.

Cowan, James C. *D. H. Lawrence and the Trembling Balance.* University Park: Pennsylvania State University Press, 1990.

———. *D. H. Lawrence: An Annotated Bibliography of Writings About Him.* 2 vols. De Kalb: Northern Illinois University Press, 1982 [vol. I], 1984 [vol. II].

———. *D. H. Lawrence's American Journey: A Study in Literature and Myth.* Cleveland, Ohio: Press of Case Western Reserve University, 1970.

Cox, James. "Pollyanalytics and Pedagogy: Teaching Lawrence's Short Stories." In "On the Teaching of D. H. Lawrence: A Forum," in *D. H. Lawrence Review* 8, no. 1 (Spring 1975): 63–79.

Critical Essays on D. H. Lawrence. Edited by Dennis Jackson and Fleda Brown Jackson. Boston: G. K. Hall, 1988.

Cushman, Keith. "The Achievement of *England, My England and Other Stories.*" In *D. H. Lawrence: The Man Who Lived,* edited by Robert B. Partlow and Harry T. Moore, 27–38. Carbondale: Southern Illinois University Press, 1980.

———. *D. H. Lawrence at Work: The Emergence of the "Prussian Officer" Stories.* Charlottesville: University Press of Virginia, 1978.

———. "The Young Lawrence and the Short Story." *Modern British Literature* 3, no. 2 (Fall 1978): 101–12.

Delavenay, Emile. *D. H. Lawrence: The Man and His Work. The Formative Years, 1885–1919.* London: William Heinemann, 1972.

A D. H. Lawrence Handbook. Edited by Keith Sagar. Totowa, N.J.: Barnes and Noble, 1982.

D. H. Lawrence: New Studies. Edited by Christopher Heywood. New York: St. Martin's Press, 1987.

D. H. Lawrence Review. 10, no. 3 (Fall 1977). Special issue: Psychoanalytic Criticism of the Short Stories.

D. H. Lawrence Review. 16, no. 3 (Fall 1983). Special issue: D. H. Lawrence's Short Fiction.

Doherty, Gerald. "The Third Encounter: Paradigms of Courtship in D. H. Lawrence's Shorter Fiction." *D. H. Lawrence Review* 17, no. 2 (Summer 1984): 135–51.

Draper, Ronald P. "The Tales." In *D. H. Lawrence,* 119–48. New York: Twayne, 1964.

Durr, Volker. "The Image of the Prussian Officer in Literature and History." In *Imperial Germany,* edited by Volker Durr, Kathy Harms, and Peter Hayes, 75–89. Madison: University of Wisconsin Press, 1985.

Elsbree, Langdon. *The Rituals of Life: Patterns in Narratives.* Port Washington, N.Y.: Kennikat Press National University Publications, 1982.

Finney, Brian. "D. H. Lawrence's Progress to Maturity: From Holograph Manuscript to Final Publication of *The Prussian Officer and Other Stories.*" *Studies in Bibliography* 28 (1975): 321–32.

————. "Introduction." In *Selected Short Stories by D. H. Lawrence*, edited by Brian Finney, 11–29. Harmondsworth, England: Penguin English Library, 1982.

Ford, George H. *Double Measure: A Study of the Novels and Stories of D. H. Lawrence.* New York: Holt, Rinehart and Winston, 1965.

Friedman, Alan. "The Other Lawrence." *Partisan Review* 37 (1970): 239–50.

Garcia, Reloy, and James Karabatsos, eds. *Concordance to the Short Fiction of D. H. Lawrence.* Lincoln: University of Nebraska Press, 1972.

Gerard, David, comp. "A Glossary of Nottinghamshire Dialect and Mining Terms." In *A D. H. Lawrence Handbook*, edited by Keith Sagar, 165–76. New York: Barnes and Noble, 1982.

Gordon, David J. *D. H. Lawrence as a Literary Critic.* New Haven, Conn.: Yale University Press, 1966.

Harris, Janice Hubbard. *The Short Fiction of D. H. Lawrence.* New Brunswick, N. J.: Rutgers University Press, 1984.

Hirsch, Gordon D. "The Laurentian Double: Images of D. H. Lawrence in the Stories." *D. H. Lawrence Review* 10, no. 3 (Fall 1977): 270–76.

Hough, Graham. *The Dark Sun: A Study of D. H. Lawrence.* London: Duckworth, 1956.

Jones, William M. "Growth of a Symbol: The Sun in Lawrence and Eudora Welty." *University of Kansas City Review* 26 (1959): 68–73.

Kalnins, Mara. "D. H. Lawrence's 'Two Marriages' and 'Daughters of the Vicar.'" *Ariel* 7 (1976): 32–49.

Kinkead-Weekes, Mark. "The Marble and the Statue: The Exploratory Imagination of D. H. Lawrence." In *Imagined Worlds: Essays on Some English Novels and Novelists in Honour of John Butt*, edited by Maynard Mack and Ian Gregor, 371–418. London: Methuen, 1968.

Krishnamurthi, M. G. *D. H. Lawrence: Tale as a Medium.* Mysore, India: Rao and Raghaven, 1970.

Lakshmi, Vijay. "Dialectic of Consciousness in the Short Fiction of Lawrence." In *Essays on D. H. Lawrence*, edited by T. R. Sharma, 125–33. Meerut, India: Shalabh Book House, 1987.

Leavis, F. R. *D. H. Lawrence: Novelist.* New York: Alfred A. Knopf, 1956.

Littlewood, J.C.F. "D. H. Lawrence's Early Tales." *Cambridge Quarterly* 1 (1966): 107–24.

Mackenzie, D. Kenneth. "Ennui and Energy in *England, My England.*" In *D. H. Lawrence: A Critical Study of the Major Novels and Other Writings*, edited by A. H. Gomme, 120–41. New York: Barnes and Noble, 1978.

MacNiven, Ian S. "D. H. Lawrence's Indian Summer." In *D. H. Lawrence: The Man Who Lived*, edited by Robert B. Partlow and Harry T. Moore, 42–46. Carbondale: Southern Illinois University Press, 1980.

Merivale, Patricia. "Culminations: D. H. Lawrence." In *Pan the Goat God: His Myth in Modern Times*, 194–219 and 273–78. Cambridge, Mass.: Harvard University Press, 1969.

Bibliography

Michaels, Jennifer E. "The Horse as Life Symbol in the Prose Works of D H. Lawrence." *International Fiction Review*, 5, no. 2 (July 1978): 116–23.

Michaels-Tonks, Jennifer. *D. H. Lawrence: The Polarity of North and South: Germany and Italy in His Prose Works*. Bonn, Germany: Bouvier, 1976.

Moore, Harry T. *D. H. Lawrence: His Life and Works*. 2d ed. New York: Twayne, 1964.

———. *The Priest of Love: A Life of D. H. Lawrence*. Rev. ed. New York: Farrar, Straus, and Giroux, 1974.

Moynahan, Joseph. *The Deed of Life: The Novels and Tales of D. H. Lawrence*. Princeton, N.J.: Princeton University Press, 1963.

———. "Foreword." In Lawrence's *A Modern Lover and Other Stories*, ix–xxiii. New York: Ballantine Books, 1969.

Nehls, Edward H. *D. H. Lawrence: A Composite Biography*. 3 vols. Madison: University of Wisconsin Press, 1957–59.

O'Connor, Frank. "The Writer Who Rode Away." In his *The Lonely Voice: A Study of the Short Story*, 143–55. Cleveland, Ohio: World Publishing, 1962.

Padhi, Bibhu. *D. H. Lawrence: Modes of Fictional Style*. Troy, N.Y.: Whitston Publishing, 1989.

Partlow, Robert B., Jr., and Harry T. Moore, eds. *D. H. Lawrence: The Man Who Lived. Papers Delivered at the D. H. Lawrence Conference at Southern Illinois University, Carbondale, April 1979*. Carbondale: Southern Illinois University Press, 1980. (Includes three articles on "Lawrence's Short Stories," 25–46.)

Piccolo, Anthony. "Ritual Strategy: Concealed Form in the Short Stories of D. H. Lawrence." *Mid-Hudson Language Studies* 2 (1979): 88–99.

Pinion, F. B. "Shorter Stories." In A *D. H. Lawrence Companion: Life, Thought, and Works*, 218–48. London: Macmillan, 1978.

Poynter, John S. "The Early Short Stories of D. H. Lawrence." In *D. H. Lawrence: The Man Who Lived*, edited by Robert B. Partlow and Harry T. Moore, 39–41. Carbondale: Southern Illinois University Press, 1980.

Pritchard, R. E. *D. H. Lawrence: Body of Darkness*. London: Hutchinson University Library, 1971.

Roberts, Warren. *A Bibliography of D. H. Lawrence*. 2d ed. Cambridge: Cambridge University Press, 1982.

Robinson, Ian. "D. H. Lawrence and English Prose." In *D. H. Lawrence: A Critical Study of the Major Novels and Other Writings*, edited by A. H. Gomme, 13–29. Sussex, England: Harvester Press, 1978.

Rose, Shirley. "Physical Trauma in D. H. Lawrence's Short Fiction." *Contemporary Literature* 16 (1975): 73–83.

Ross, Donald, Jr. "Who's Talking? How Characters Become Narrators in Fiction." *Modern Language Notes* 91 (1976): 1222–42.

Rossman, Charles. "Myth and Misunderstanding D. H. Lawrence." In *Twenti-eth-Century Poetry, Fiction, Theory,* edited by Harry R. Garvin, 81–101. Cranbury, N.J.: Bucknell University Press, 1977.

Ruderman, Judith. *D. H. Lawrence and the Devouring Mother: The Search for a Patriarchal Ideal of Leadership.* Durham, N.C.: Duke University Press, 1984.

Sagar, Keith. *The Art of D. H. Lawrence.* Cambridge: Cambridge University Press, 1966.

———. *D. H. Lawrence: A Calendar of His Works.* (With a Checklist of the Manuscripts of D. H. Lawrence by Lindeth Vasey.) Austin: The University of Texas Press, 1979.

———. *D. H. Lawrence: Life into Art.* Athens: University of Georgia Press, 1985.

Scott, James F. "D. H. Lawrence's *Germania:* Ethnic Psychology and Cultural Crisis in the Shorter Fiction." *D. H. Lawrence Review* 10 (1977): 142–64.

Serraillier, Ian. "Introduction." In Lawrence's *Selected Tales,* vii–xi. London: Heinemann, 1963.

Sharma, Susheel Kumar. "Antifeminism in D. H. Lawrence's Short Stories." In *Essays on D. H. Lawrence,* edited by T. R. Sharma, 139–46. Meerut, India: Shalabh Book House, 1987.

Shaw, Valerie. *The Short Story: A Critical Introduction.* London: Longman, 1983.

Siegel, Carol. "Virginia Woolf's and Katherine Mansfield's Responses to D. H. Lawrence's Fiction." *D. H. Lawrence Review* 21, no. 3 (Fall 1989): 291–311.

Slade, Tony. "The Short Novels and the Stories." In his *D. H. Lawrence,* 95–113. New York: Arco Publishing, 1970.

Stewart, J.I.M. "Lawrence." In *Eight Modern Writers.* Oxford: Clarendon Press, 1963.

Tedlock, E. W., Jr. *D. H. Lawrence: Artist and Rebel. A Study of Lawrence's Fiction.* Albuquerque: University of New Mexico Press, 1963.

Temple, J. "The Definition of Innocence: A Consideration of the Short Stories of D. H. Lawrence." *Studia Germanica Gandensia* 20 (1979): 105–18.

Travis, Leigh. "D. H. Lawrence: The Blood-Conscious Artist." *American Imago* 25 (1968): 163–90.

Van DerVeen, Berend K. *The Development of D. H. Lawrence's Prose Themes, 1906–1915.* (Groningen: University of Groningen, 1983.

Van Spanckeren, Kathryn. "Lawrence and the Uses of Story." *D. H. Lawrence Review* 18, nos. 2–3 (Summer/Fall 1985–1986): 291–300.

Vickery, John B. "D. H. Lawrence: The Mythic Elements." In *The Literary Impact of the Golden Bough,* 294–325. Princeton, N.J.: Princeton University Press, 1973.

Welty, Eudora. "The Reading and Writing of Short Stories." *Atlantic Monthly,* February 1949, pp. 54–57, and March 1949, pp. 46–49.

Weiss, Daniel A. *Oedipus in Nottingham: D. H. Lawrence.* Seattle: University of Washington Press, 1962.

West, Anthony. *D. H. Lawrence.* London: Arthur Barker, 1950. See especially Chapter 7, 83–105.

Widmer, Kingsley. *The Art of Perversity: D. H. Lawrence's Shorter Fictions.* Seattle: University of Washington Press, 1962.

Wilt, Judith. "D. H. Lawrence: Ghosts in the Daylight." In *Ghosts of the Gothic: Austen, Eliot, and Lawrence,* 231–92. Princeton: Princeton University Press, 1980.

Worthen, John. *D. H. Lawrence.* London: Edward Arnold, 1991.

———. *D. H. Lawrence: The Early Years 1885–1912.* Cambridge: Cambridge University Press, 1991.

———. "Short Story and Autobiography: Kinds of Detachment in D. H. Lawrence's Early Fiction." *Renaissance and Modern Studies* 29 (1985): 1–15. A special issue entitled *D. H. Lawrence 1885–1930,* edited by James T. Boulton.

Zytaruk, George J. *D. H. Lawrence's Response to Russian Literature.* The Hague, The Netherlands: Mouton, 1971.

INDEX

The Author

Weldon Thornton is professor of English at the University of North Carolina at Chapel Hill. He is the author of *Allusions in Ulysses: An Annotated List* and *J. M. Synge and the Western Mind*. He is also the co-editor of *Joyce's Ulysses: The Larger Perspective*. In 1987 he was a Fulbright lecturer in Belo Horizonte, Brazil. During the years 1982–85, he was Bowman and Gordon Gray Professor of English at the University of North Carolina at Chapel Hill.

The Editor

General Editor Gordon Weaver earned his B.A. in English at the University of Wisconsin-Milwaukee in 1961; his M.A. in English at the University of Illinois, where he studied as a Woodrow Wilson Fellow, in 1962; and his Ph.D. in English and creative writing at the University of Denver in 1970. He is author of several novels, including *Count a Lonely Cadence, Give Him a Stone, Circling Byzantium,* and most recently *The Eight Corners of the World* (1988). Many of his numerous short stories are collected in *The Entombed Man of Thule, Such Waltzing Was Not Easy, Getting Serious, Morality Play, A World Quite Round,* and *Men Who Would Be Good* (1991). Recognition of his fiction includes the St. Lawrence Award for Fiction (1973), two National Endowment for the Arts Fellowships (1974, 1989), and the O. Henry First Prize (1979). He edited *The American Short Story, 1945–1980: A Critical History,* and is currently editor of *Cimarron Review.* He is professor of English at Oklahoma State University. Married, and the father of three daughters, he lives in Stillwater, Oklahoma.